LEVITICUS
FROM START2FINISH

MICHAEL WHITWORTH

© 2025 by Start2Finish

All rights reserved. No part of this publication may be reproduced, stored in a retrieval system, or transmitted in any form or by any means without the prior written permission of the author. The only exception is brief quotations in printed reviews.

ISBN 978-1-944704-17-9

Published by Start2Finish
Bend, Oregon 97702
start2finish.org

Printed in the United States of America

Unless otherwise noted, all Scripture quotations are from The Holy Bible, English Standard Version®, copyright © 2001 by Crossway Bibles, a publishing ministry of Good News Publishers. Used by permission. All rights reserved.

Cover Design: Evangela Creative

CONTENTS

1.	Draw Near	5
2.	The Price of Forgiveness	13
3.	Set Apart to Serve	21
4.	Holy Bodies, Holy Birth	29
5.	Contagious Defilement	39
6.	The Day of Atonement	49
7.	The Holiness Code	59
8.	Sacred Service	67
9.	Holy Time	77
10.	Light, Bread, & Blasphemy	87
11.	Freedom & Rest	97
12.	Blessing & Commitment	105

1

DRAW NEAR

LEVITICUS 1-3

Objective: To understand how Israel's offerings taught devotion, gratitude, and fellowship with a holy God.

INTRODUCTION

When the smoke rose from an Israelite altar, it carried more than the scent of burning flesh—it carried a story. Imagine a shepherd walking from his tent before dawn, leading a spotless ram through the desert mist. He approaches the tabernacle, heart pounding, aware that every step brings him closer to the presence of God. This isn't superstition; it's worship. He lays his hand on the animal's head, confesses his sins, and watches as life drains away—his life, offered through another. The smell of sacrifice fills the air, and strangely, it is called a "pleasing aroma."

Leviticus opens with that scene. God has chosen to dwell among his people, but fellowship with a holy God requires holiness from them. The first three chapters describe offerings of devotion, gratitude, and peace—the foundation of all worship. These sacrifices were not mere ceremony; they were invitations. Through them, God taught Israel how to draw near, how to honor him, and how to live in his presence.

Before the thunder of Sinai faded, the Lord called again—not to terrify but to invite: "When any one of you brings an offering…" (Lev. 1:2). The way to holiness begins with an open door and a burning altar.

EXAMINATION

A God who invites his people near (1:1)

Leviticus opens where Exodus left off—with the glory of the Lord filling the tabernacle (Exod. 40:34–35). The book begins, "The Lord called Moses and spoke to him from the tent of meeting." The word "called" (Hebrew *qārā'*) signals invitation and instruction. Though the tabernacle now stood completed, the question from Exodus remained: how can sinful people approach a holy God? Leviticus provides the answer.

In the ancient world, sacrifices were common, but Israel's system was unique in purpose. Pagan offerings sought to feed or appease deities; Israel's sacrifices expressed gratitude, repentance, and fellowship with the living God who had already redeemed them. Worship did not earn favor—it responded to grace. Each offering in chapters 1–3 reveals a dimension of that relationship.

The burnt offering – total devotion (1:2–17)

The burnt offering was the most frequent and comprehensive sacrifice. It could be drawn from the herd, the flock, or birds, making it accessible to all Israelites. The worshiper personally brought the animal to the entrance of the tent, laid his hand on its head, and slaughtered it before the Lord. This symbolic act identified the animal as his substitute. The life of the worshiper was figuratively transferred to the victim; its blood represented atonement on his behalf (1:4).

The animal was then flayed, cut into pieces, and completely consumed on the altar. Nothing was eaten. Unlike other offerings where portions were shared, the burnt offering was wholly given to God—a "pleasing aroma to the Lord" (1:9, 13, 17). This phrase, recurring throughout Leviticus, does not suggest that God enjoys the smell of smoke but that he accepts the worshiper's devotion. The aroma of obedience delights him.

The full consumption of the animal expressed total surrender. The worshiper held nothing back. Even the priest received no portion. In this, the offering mirrored the call of discipleship—"present your bodies as a living sacrifice, holy and acceptable to God" (Rom. 12:1). Christians, too, are called to a whole-burnt life of devotion, where everything belongs to God.

Leviticus emphasizes detail—the kind of animal, how it is flayed, how its entrails are washed. These particulars underscore God's concern for order and purity in worship. Approaching him casually or carelessly dishonors his holiness. The worshiper's meticulous obedience declared reverence, not ritualism.

The inclusion of birds for the poor (1:14–17) shows God's compassion. Holiness did not depend on wealth. Whether a bull or a pigeon, the sacrifice was "accepted for him to make atonement" (1:4). Grace equalized every worshiper before the altar.

The grain offering – grateful dedication (2:1–16)

While chapter 1 centers on blood, chapter 2 centers on bread. The grain offering often accompanied burnt or peace offerings. It expressed gratitude for God's provision and consecration of one's daily labor. The offering could be raw flour, baked bread, or fried cakes, but always "fine flour" mixed with oil and frankincense (2:1). Every element carried symbolic weight—oil for richness and vitality, frankincense for joy and fragrance, and fine flour for purity of effort.

No leaven or honey was to be included (2:11), for both ferment and decay. Holiness tolerates no corruption. Instead, every offering required salt (2:13), "the salt of the covenant with your God." Salt preserved and purified; it symbolized faithfulness. In covenant language, salt represented enduring loyalty—an unspoiled relationship with God.

A portion of the grain offering was burned on the altar as "a memorial portion" (2:2, 9). The rest was eaten by the priests in a holy place, signifying shared fellowship between God and his servants. Thus, while the burnt offering represented total surrender, the grain offering depicted ongoing service—daily life devoted to God's glory.

For Christians, the principle endures: holiness is not confined to sacrifice but saturates ordinary work. Paul's command echoes Leviticus—"whatever you do, in word or deed, do everything in the name of the Lord Jesus" (Col. 3:17). Bringing the "grain" of our labor to God turns routine into worship.

The peace offering – fellowship and joy (3:1-17)

The peace offering was the most joyful of all. Derived from *shalom*, it celebrated wholeness, harmony, and restored relationship. Unlike the burnt offering, only portions of this sacrifice were burned; the remainder was eaten in a communal meal shared by the worshiper, his family, and the priests. Fellowship with God overflowed into fellowship with others.

Leviticus describes three types of peace offerings: for thanksgiving (7:12-15), for fulfillment of a vow (7:16), and for freewill devotion. The animal—bull, sheep, or goat—had to be without blemish. Blood was again sprinkled on the altar, symbolizing atonement as the foundation of peace. Fat portions, considered the richest parts, were offered to God (3:3-5, 9-11, 14-16). The repeated warning not to eat the fat or blood (3:17) preserved the sanctity of life as God's gift.

In the ancient world, shared meals sealed covenants. Here, Israel dined with God. The peace offering foreshadowed the table fellowship Christians now enjoy in Christ. Our communion meal each Lord's Day recalls the same reality—the blood that made peace (Eph. 2:13-14) and the joy of fellowship within the family of faith.

The peace offering was never coerced. It arose from gratitude and delight. The worshiper did not offer to gain peace but because peace already existed. In the same way, Christians partake of the Lord's Supper not to earn grace but to celebrate it.

The structure of worship

Leviticus 1-3 reveals a progression: atonement → dedication → fellowship. Sin is dealt with, life is consecrated, and communion follows. The order is deliberate. One cannot enjoy peace with God without first being cleansed and committed. The pattern anticipates the gospel—justification through sacrifice, sanctification through service, and fellowship through grace.

The detailed procedures also reinforce God's initiative. Each chapter begins, "When any one of you brings an offering to the Lord…" (1:2; 2:1; 3:1). The Hebrew term for "offering," *qorbān*, literally means "that which draws near." Sacrifice was never about keeping God away but about coming close. Holiness is relational. God desires nearness, not distance.

Furthermore, Leviticus sanctified the physical world. Animals, grain, oil, and salt—ordinary materials—became instruments of worship. In doing so, God taught Israel that all creation can be redeemed for his glory. Worship is embodied; holiness is lived.

Christ, the true offering

Every offering in Leviticus points beyond itself. The burnt offering anticipated Christ's total surrender: "He gave himself up for us, a fragrant offering and sacrifice to God" (Eph. 5:2). The grain offering foreshadowed his perfect obedience—"My food is to do the will of him who sent me" (John 4:34). The peace offering culminated in his reconciling death: "having made peace by the blood of his cross" (Col. 1:20).

In Christ, the sequence is complete. He is both priest and victim, offering and fellowship. Through his sacrifice, we draw near "with a true heart in full assurance of faith" (Heb. 10:22). The old altars are gone, but the principle remains—worship demands holiness, gratitude, and joy.

Holiness as relationship

Leviticus is often caricatured as cold ritual, yet its opening chapters reveal intimacy. God does not speak from Sinai's thunder but from the tent of meeting, dwelling among his people. Each offering provided a way to maintain that closeness. Holiness is the vocabulary of relationship.

Modern believers may not slaughter animals, but we still offer ourselves—our time, work, words, and resources—as living sacrifices. The altar has moved from the courtyard to the heart. When we give, serve, pray, and praise, we mirror Israel's ancient gestures of devotion.

Holiness, therefore, is not distance from the world but nearness to God that transforms how we live within it.

APPLICATION

1. Worship requires wholehearted devotion

The burnt offering teaches that drawing near to God means surrendering everything. The entire animal was consumed, symbolizing complete consecration. Modern believers cannot offer half-hearted worship or compartmentalized obedience. God deserves our best time, attention, and affection—not the leftovers of convenience. When we approach him in prayer, song, or service, we bring ourselves to the altar. Paul captured this principle:

"present your bodies as a living sacrifice" (Rom. 12:1). True worship isn't measured by the quality of the singing or the power of the moment but by the depth of our daily devotion. God still delights in a "pleasing aroma"—a life that is fully his.

2. Gratitude turns work into worship

The grain offering reminds us that holiness extends into the ordinary. Israel offered flour, oil, and salt—the fruit of daily labor—as acts of thanksgiving. Christians, too, glorify God not only in the assembly but also in the workplace, the classroom, and the home. Every task becomes sacred when done in gratitude. Whether we farm, teach, build, or parent, we lay our "grain" before the Lord. Colossians 3:17 urges us to do everything in the name of Jesus, giving thanks to God. Holiness is not escape from daily life but consecration within it. Worship is a rhythm of thankfulness that sanctifies routine.

3. Peace with God creates peace with others

The peace offering celebrated fellowship—a shared meal between the worshiper, the priest, and God. Redemption was never meant to be solitary. Reconciliation with God transforms relationships among his people. At the Lord's table, Christians proclaim that hostility has ended; forgiveness flows both vertically and horizontally. Grudges, bitterness, and pride cannot survive where Christ's blood has made peace (Eph. 2:13–14). If we wish to enjoy communion with God, we must extend it to others. Every Sunday meal around the Lord's Supper is a miniature peace offering—a declaration that love and unity reign among those redeemed.

4. God welcomes every worshiper

Leviticus opens with compassion: whether one brought a bull, a lamb, or a pigeon, each sacrifice was acceptable. Holiness was not priced by income but offered through faith. God's grace levels all distinctions of wealth and status. The same remains true today. The widow's mite, the student's time, the elderly believer's quiet prayer—all rise before God as a pleasing aroma. Worship is not about grandeur but sincerity. What matters is not the size of the gift but the heart behind it. The God who welcomed the poor man's dove still receives the humble soul who comes near through Christ.

CONCLUSION

Leviticus begins not with distance, but with invitation. God called his people to draw near through sacrifice, teaching them that holiness and fellowship are gifts, not achievements. The burnt, grain, and peace offerings formed a pattern of relationship—atonement, dedication, and communion—that still echoes in Christian worship. At the cross, Jesus became our perfect offering, our fragrant sacrifice, our lasting peace. Through him, believers approach the throne without fear. The fire that once burned on Israel's altar now burns in grateful hearts.

Next, Leviticus 4–7 will deepen this picture, revealing how sin disrupts fellowship and how God provides atonement to restore it.

REFLECTION

1. What does the word "offering" (*qorbān*) teach about God's desire for nearness?
2. Why was the burnt offering completely consumed on the altar?
3. How did the grain offering reflect everyday gratitude and faithfulness?
4. In what ways did the peace offering symbolize restored fellowship?
5. How do the details of each sacrifice reveal God's holiness?
6. How does Christ fulfill the meaning of all three offerings?

DISCUSSION

1. What does wholehearted devotion look like in modern worship?
2. How can gratitude transform your daily work into worship?
3. What habits help maintain peace with others in the church?
4. Why is shared fellowship vital to spiritual maturity?
5. How can the church ensure that worship is inclusive of all Christians?
6. Which offering most challenges or inspires your faith today and why?

2

THE PRICE OF FORGIVENESS
LEVITICUS 4–7

Objective: To discover how the sin and guilt offerings reveal sin's cost and God's mercy.

INTRODUCTION

A few years ago, a museum in Italy displayed an ancient marble statue with a small sign: "Please do not touch." Yet fingerprints soon appeared on its smooth surface, and over time the oils from countless hands left the stone discolored. The guards hadn't noticed, and no single visitor caused the damage—but the result was undeniable. What began as harmless curiosity became lasting defilement.

Sin works the same way. We may not mean to offend, but unintentional touches of pride, envy, or deceit stain what is holy. Leviticus 4–7 confronts this uncomfortable truth: even the sins we don't plan still need forgiveness. The God who dwells among his people is too pure to ignore pollution, yet too merciful to abandon the guilty.

In these chapters, Israel learns that atonement has a price. Blood must be shed, restitution made, and holiness restored. Through every bull, goat, and ram, God taught his people the cost of cleansing—and pointed forward to the day when his Son would pay it fully. Forgiveness is free, but it is never cheap.

EXAMINATION

Sin has a cost (4:1-2)

Leviticus turns from offerings of devotion to offerings of forgiveness. The first three chapters taught Israel how to draw near; chapters 4-7 reveal what to do when that fellowship is broken. The Lord spoke to Moses, saying, "Speak to the people of Israel, saying, If anyone sins unintentionally..." (4:1-2). Sin, whether deliberate or accidental, disrupts the holiness that allows God to dwell among his people. The solution is not denial or despair but atonement.

These chapters describe two related sacrifices—the sin offering and the guilt offering—each teaching the cost of sin and the grace of forgiveness. Together they form the heart of Leviticus' theology: sin separates, blood reconciles, and holiness restores. The rituals may seem foreign, but their message endures—every act of forgiveness depends on a substitute's life in the sinner's place.

The sin offering – cleansing for the guilty (4:3-5:13)

The sin offering addressed sins committed "unintentionally," that is, without deliberate rebellion but still violating God's command. Ignorance did not erase guilt; holiness demanded atonement. Four cases are described, each determined by status: the anointed priest (4:3-12), the whole congregation (4:13-21), a leader (4:22-26), and a common person (4:27-35). The higher one's position, the greater the consequence, because sin in leadership spreads impurity to others.

When the anointed priest sinned, his guilt "brought guilt on the people" (4:3). A bull was required—costly, large, and pure. The priest laid his hand on the animal's head, slaughtered it, and carried its blood into the tent of meeting, sprinkling it before the veil and placing some on the horns of the incense altar. The rest was poured out at the base of the bronze altar. The carcass was burned outside the camp, symbolizing removal of defilement from God's presence.

When the entire congregation sinned, the ritual was similar. Corporate sin required corporate repentance. Leaders, however, brought a male goat, and commoners, a female goat or lamb—less costly but still valuable. The pattern taught personal responsibility before God and the equal need for cleansing.

The laying on of hands dramatized substitution. The worshiper identified with the victim; its death became his death. Blood, representing life, was God's chosen means of atonement: "for it is the blood that makes atonement by the life" (17:11). The sprinkling of blood purified both sinner and sanctuary, cleansing the space where holiness and humanity met.

In Leviticus 5:1-13, the law expanded to cover specific offenses—failure to testify, contact with impurity, rash oaths—and provided an option for the poor: two turtledoves or pigeons, and for the destitute, a small measure of fine flour. Even the poorest Israelite could find forgiveness. God's mercy reached from priest to pauper, ensuring that no one was too insignificant to be cleansed.

The sin offering reveals two truths that echo through Scripture: sin contaminates what is holy, and forgiveness costs life. Hebrews later declares that "without the shedding of blood there is no forgiveness of sins" (Heb. 9:22). The cross would embody that principle fully—Christ's life poured out as the true sin offering for all.

The guilt offering – restitution and restoration (5:14-6:7)

Closely related to the sin offering, the guilt offering focused on sins that violated sacred things or defrauded others. It emphasized restitution—the tangible repayment of what was lost. Sin not only offends God but also damages relationships and property; grace requires setting things right.

If someone misused holy items, withheld offerings, or unintentionally violated a command, he was to bring a ram "without blemish out of the flock" and add restitution equal to the loss plus one-fifth more (5:15-16). Forgiveness was not abstract—it required action. Repentance demanded restoration.

The same principle applied to sins against others (6:1-7). If a person deceived a neighbor in a matter of trust, stole property, or swore falsely, he had to return what was taken, add twenty percent, and then bring a guilt offering to the priest. Only then would "the priest make atonement for him before the Lord, and he shall be forgiven" (6:7).

In the gospel, Zacchaeus reaffirmed this principle when he told Jesus, "If I have defrauded anyone of anything, I restore it fourfold" (Luke 19:8). True repentance changes behavior and seeks reconciliation. The guilt offering teaches that grace never excuses injustice—it repairs it.

Christ fulfilled this pattern perfectly. Isaiah foresaw that the Servant would make "his soul an offering for guilt" (Isa. 53:10). Jesus bore not only our moral debt but also the full restitution of what sin had stolen—peace with God and righteousness for humanity.

The law of the offerings (6:8–7:38)

The final section of this unit revisits the burnt, grain, sin, and guilt offerings, this time from the priest's perspective. The focus shifts from the worshiper's need for forgiveness to the priest's responsibility to maintain holiness. The fire on the altar was never to go out (6:12–13), symbolizing continual devotion. Day and night, the priest tended the flame—an image of ongoing intercession that pointed toward the ceaseless ministry of Christ.

The Burnt Offering (6:8–13). The priest arranged the wood, laid the parts in order, and removed the ashes, wearing linen garments of purity. Even waste from the sacrifice was handled reverently. Holiness leaves no part of life untouched.

The Grain Offering (6:14–23). A portion was burned as a memorial, while the rest fed the priests. Their sustenance came from the altar, showing that those who serve God live from his provision. The daily offering of fine flour at the priest's ordination (6:19–23) was wholly consumed, underscoring total dedication to God's service.

The Sin and Guilt Offerings (6:24–7:10). These sacrifices belonged entirely to the Lord, yet priests who mediated forgiveness could eat the remaining meat in a holy place. Consuming the offering symbolized participation in its holiness—sharing in the atonement God provided. But if any blood entered the sanctuary, the flesh was burned instead. The balance between privilege and reverence was delicate; mishandling holy things brought death, as Nadab and Abihu would soon learn (10:1–2).

The Peace Offering (7:11–36). The peace offering's regulations added thanksgiving loaves, timing limits, and purity requirements. The meal had to be eaten quickly—within one or two days—lest corruption defile what was holy. Gratitude demanded urgency. The law ends with the repeated prohibition: "You shall eat no fat, nor any blood" (7:23–27). Life belonged to God alone; his holiness governed even the diet of celebration.

The section concludes with a formal summary: "This is the law of the burnt offering, of the grain offering, of the sin offering, of the guilt offering, of the ordination offering, and of the peace offering" (7:37). Worship was not haphazard—it was ordered, precise, and purposeful. Through obedience, Israel learned reverence; through sacrifice, they found forgiveness.

The meaning behind the rituals

Modern readers may find these chapters repetitive or distant, yet they teach timeless truths. First, sin is serious. Even unintentional failure required blood. Holiness is not about good intentions but faithful obedience. Sin pollutes what is sacred and must be cleansed.

Second, forgiveness is costly. Every act of atonement demanded life. Each bleating lamb and slain bull reminded Israel that sin's wages are death. Grace was never cheap.

Third, forgiveness is graciously available. From the high priest to the poorest Israelite, God made a way. His mercy was not earned by sacrifice but expressed through it. The altar was a place of divine generosity.

Finally, forgiveness is transformative. The guilt offering's restitution principle reminds believers that repentance restores relationships, repairs harm, and renews community trust. True holiness is relational—it heals what sin has broken.

Christ and the cost of atonement

The New Testament repeatedly returns to Leviticus 4–7 to explain the cross. Jesus fulfilled both the sin and guilt offerings. Paul declares, "For our sake he made him to be sin who knew no sin, so that in him we might become the righteousness of God" (2 Cor. 5:21). On the cross, Christ bore not only the penalty of guilt but also its pollution. His blood purifies the conscience "from dead works to serve the living God" (Heb. 9:14).

Unlike the priests who offered daily sacrifices, Jesus offered himself "once for all" (Heb. 10:10). The fire of the altar no longer burns, because his offering is sufficient forever. Yet the principle endures: forgiveness costs life, and that life was his.

Through his death, Christ became both priest and victim. He carried our sins "outside the camp" (Heb. 13:12), echoing the burnt remains of the sin offering removed from the tabernacle precincts. He made restitution for humanity's rebellion, not with silver or gold, but with his own precious blood (1 Pet. 1:18–19). In him, justice and mercy meet perfectly.

Living in the light of forgiveness

For Israel, these sacrifices marked the rhythm of grace—confession, substitution, and cleansing. For Christians, the rhythm continues through confession, repentance, and renewed fellowship in Christ. While the altars of Leviticus have vanished, the need they addressed remains: sin separates, and only God can restore.

Every time Christians confess their sins and remember the cross, they echo the rituals of Leviticus 4–7. The difference is finality. What was once repeated daily is now remembered weekly. The table of the Lord replaces the altar of the priest. Bread and cup proclaim the same truth: forgiveness has a price, and Jesus paid it completely.

Holiness still matters. Grace does not diminish obedience; it empowers it. Those who have been cleansed are called to keep the fire of devotion burning, just as the priests kept the altar flame alive. Forgiveness is not a finish line but a beginning—the invitation to live gratefully within the presence of a holy God.

APPLICATION

1. Sin is never small

Leviticus insists that even unintentional sin requires atonement. God's holiness leaves no room for moral shortcuts or hidden faults. We live in a culture that minimizes wrongdoing, calling sin "mistakes" or "flaws." Scripture will not allow that. Every failure offends a holy God and disrupts our fellowship with him. The message of the sin offering is simple: sin matters. But grace matters more. When believers confess, the same God who demanded holiness provides cleansing through Christ's blood (1 John 1:7–9). The seriousness of sin deepens our gratitude for forgiveness.

2. Forgiveness is costly but freely given

Each sacrifice in Leviticus required life. Bulls, goats, and lambs all testified that "the wages of sin is death" (Rom. 6:23). Forgiveness has a price—always has, always will. Yet the gospel turns the old pattern inside out. Instead of the sinner bringing a substitute, the Substitute brings himself. Jesus fulfills every altar and every priesthood. Remembering that truth keeps grace from becoming cheap. When we realize what forgiveness cost, worship becomes reverent and obedience becomes joyful. The cross is not a loophole in justice but its fulfillment.

3. True repentance restores what sin damaged

The guilt offering demanded restitution: pay back what was taken, plus one-fifth more. God's grace forgives freely but expects integrity. Repentance means more than regret—it means repair. The thief returns what he stole; the liar makes the truth known; the gossip rebuilds trust. Genuine repentance includes restitution. Christians who understand the guilt offering see grace not as permission to forget the past but as power to make it right. Forgiveness heals the heart, but repentance mends the harm.

4. Forgiven people keep the fire burning

The priests were told, "The fire on the altar shall be kept burning; it shall not go out" (Lev. 6:13). That flame symbolized constant devotion—a reminder that grace must be tended daily. God has forgiven us completely, but holiness still requires attention. Prayer, Scripture, worship, and service keep the embers of gratitude alive. Neglect cools the heart; discipline keeps it aflame. The Christian's life should smell like the altar—faithful, enduring, and pleasing to God. Forgiveness is not the end of worship; it is its beginning.

CONCLUSION

The smoke of Leviticus 4–7 rises with a sobering message—sin always costs life. Every drop of blood, every burning carcass, reminded Israel that forgiveness is never free. Yet behind the altar stood mercy. God did not demand sacrifice to crush his people but to cleanse them, making fellowship possible again. The sin and guilt offerings pointed beyond themselves to the cross, where the perfect substitute bore guilt and paid the debt once and for all.

For Christians, every remembrance of the Lord's Supper echoes those ancient rituals. We come not with animals but with gratitude, knowing the price of forgiveness has been paid.

Next, Leviticus 8–10 will reveal how God's priests were set apart to serve—and what happens when holiness is ignored.

REFLECTION

1. Why did even unintentional sins require a sacrifice in Israel's law?
2. What does laying hands on the animal symbolize in the sin offering?
3. How did the guilt offering combine forgiveness with restitution?
4. Why was the altar fire never allowed to go out?
5. How do these sacrifices foreshadow Jesus' atonement on the cross?
6. What do these chapters teach about God's justice and mercy working together?

DISCUSSION

1. How do we sometimes minimize the seriousness of sin today?
2. What does it mean that forgiveness is free but never cheap?
3. How can repentance include practical restitution in modern life?
4. What disciplines help you "keep the fire burning" in your faith?
5. Why should awareness of sin deepen, not diminish, our joy in Christ?
6. How does gratitude for forgiveness shape the way you treat others?

3

SET APART TO SERVE
LEVITICUS 8–10

Objective: To recognize the holiness required for God's servants and its fulfillment in Christ's priesthood.

INTRODUCTION

Years ago, a man touring Buckingham Palace accidentally stepped past the velvet rope meant to keep visitors at a respectful distance. Within seconds, a guard's firm voice filled the hall: "Step back, sir." The boundary wasn't cruelty—it was reverence. Some places require more than casual entry.

Leviticus 8–10 opens the door to such holy space. Israel's priests were being set apart to serve in the very presence of God. Their garments shimmered with gold thread, their hands were wet with oil and blood, and their hearts surely trembled. They would stand between heaven and earth, offering sacrifices on behalf of the people. But this sacred privilege came with danger. One careless act could profane the holy and invite death.

These chapters show both the wonder and the weight of worship. Holiness isn't an accessory to ministry—it's the foundation. God's priests were chosen, cleansed, and commissioned not to perform rituals but to reflect his glory. Through their story, believers learn what it means to serve a God who is near, yet never common.

EXAMINATION

A holy calling (8:1–5)

Leviticus 8–10 describes a turning point in Israel's story. The tabernacle had been built, the offerings explained, and now the priests who would serve in God's presence had to be consecrated. Moses gathered Aaron, his sons, and the entire congregation at the entrance of the tent of meeting, saying, "This is the thing that the Lord has commanded to be done" (8:5).

Priesthood was not a personal career choice; it was a divine calling. The Lord appointed Aaron and his descendants to stand between a holy God and a sinful nation. This moment was not merely a ceremony—it was the inauguration of ministry, the opening of Israel's worship life. Through their hands, Israel's sacrifices would rise, and through their intercession, sin would be forgiven. Every act, every robe, every anointing symbolized the gravity of standing in God's presence on behalf of others.

Consecration of the priests (8:6–36)

The consecration ceremony in chapter 8 unfolds like a sacred drama with seven scenes: washing, clothing, anointing, sacrifice, sprinkling, ordination, and fellowship. Each step communicated one truth—holiness must be conferred before ministry can begin.

Washed with Water (8:6). Before Aaron and his sons could serve, they were washed at the entrance of the tent. Cleansing came first. The priest could not mediate purity for others while defiled himself. The water symbolized moral and spiritual cleansing—a reminder that those who approach God must be made clean by God.

Clothed for Glory and Beauty (8:7–9). Moses dressed Aaron in the priestly garments described in Exodus 28: the tunic, robe, ephod, breastpiece, and turban with the golden plate inscribed "Holy to the Lord." Each piece displayed dignity and purpose. The ephod's stones bore the names of Israel's tribes—signifying that the priest carried the people on his shoulders and over his heart. Ministry was intercession, not self-display.

Anointed for Service (8:10–13). Moses anointed the tabernacle, its furnishings, and Aaron himself with oil, marking them as God's possession. The fragrant oil symbolized the Spirit's presence and empowerment.

Aaron's sons were clothed and anointed after him, signifying participation in his office but under his authority.

Sacrificed for Atonement (8:14–29). Three offerings followed: the sin offering (for cleansing), the burnt offering (for dedication), and the ordination offering (for consecration). Moses placed blood on Aaron's right ear, thumb, and big toe—symbols of hearing, doing, and walking in obedience. A priest's entire life was to be devoted to God's service.

Finally, portions of the ordination ram and unleavened bread were waved before the Lord and then eaten by the priests, completing the ritual with fellowship. For seven days Aaron and his sons remained at the entrance of the tent, fulfilling the ordination period. Only after those days were complete could they begin their ministry.

The consecration ceremony reminded Israel that holiness is never assumed. God chooses, cleanses, and commissions those who serve him. It is not merit but mercy that places anyone in his service.

The beginning of ministry (9:1–24)

On the eighth day—the day of new beginnings—the newly consecrated priests began their first official service. Moses instructed Aaron to offer a sin offering and a burnt offering for himself, and then sacrifices for the people: a sin offering, burnt offering, grain offering, and peace offering (9:1–4). These correspond to the earlier chapters, now enacted under priestly leadership. The goal: "for today the Lord will appear to you" (9:4).

Aaron obeyed precisely. He slaughtered the calf for his own sin offering, then the people's goat, presenting each in turn as Moses directed. As the blood was sprinkled and the fat burned, the congregation watched silently. The priest who once needed cleansing now mediated cleansing for others. When the ritual concluded, "Aaron lifted up his hands toward the people and blessed them" (9:22). Together with Moses, he entered the tent of meeting and came out to bless the people again. Then it happened: "The glory of the Lord appeared to all the people, and fire came out from before the Lord and consumed the burnt offering on the altar" (9:23–24).

The consuming fire signified divine approval. God accepted their service and revealed his presence in power. The people shouted and fell on their faces in worship. This was Israel's first true day of priestly ministry—a glimpse of heaven touching earth.

For the Christian, the scene foreshadows Pentecost. Just as fire confirmed God's presence on the altar, so tongues of fire confirmed his presence among the apostles. In both cases, divine fire authenticated divine service. When worship aligns with God's command, his glory fills the space.

The sin of Nadab and Abihu (10:1–7)

The joy of chapter 9 quickly gives way to tragedy in chapter 10. "Now Nadab and Abihu, the sons of Aaron, each took his censer and put fire in it and laid incense on it and offered unauthorized fire before the Lord, which he had not commanded them" (10:1). These were not pagans but priests—men who had just witnessed God's glory. Yet in a moment of arrogance or carelessness, they disregarded divine instruction.

Fire came out again from before the Lord—but this time not to bless. "And the fire consumed them, and they died before the Lord" (10:2). The same holiness that brings life to the obedient brings death to the presumptuous. Moses explained to Aaron, "Among those who are near me I will be sanctified, and before all the people I will be glorified" (10:3). Holiness is not negotiable.

Aaron's response was silence. His heart must have been torn, yet he submitted to the justice of God. Moses commanded the removal of the bodies and instructed Aaron and his remaining sons not to mourn publicly. The priests represented the people before God; their grief could not compromise their duty. The message was clear: sacred service demands reverence.

The narrative of Nadab and Abihu stands as one of Scripture's sharpest warnings against self-willed worship. God does not accept innovation in the place of obedience. When he specifies how he is to be approached, deviation dishonors his holiness. The church redeemed by Christ holds this conviction—worship must be governed by divine authority, not human creativity. "Unauthorized fire" is any worship not commanded by God.

Instructions for priestly conduct (10:8–20)

After the tragedy, the Lord spoke directly to Aaron for the first time in the book (10:8–11). The timing is striking—after judgment comes clarification. God commanded that priests abstain from wine or strong drink when entering the tent of meeting, "that you may distinguish between the holy and the common, and between the unclean and the clean" (10:10). Sobriety was essential to discernment. The priest who represented God had to think clearly and act faithfully.

Moses then reminded Aaron and his surviving sons, Eleazar and Ithamar, to eat the remaining portions of the grain and peace offerings in a holy place (10:12–15). Yet when Moses later discovered that the sin offering's meat had been burned instead of eaten, he became angry (10:16–18). Aaron calmly explained that in light of the tragedy, it would not have been right to eat the sacrifice that day. Moses accepted his reasoning, and the chapter ends with restored order.

This closing scene highlights balance. Holiness is not mindless ritual but reverent obedience guided by wisdom. Aaron's response shows that God values discernment born of fear and faith. Holiness is relational—honoring God's command while understanding his heart.

The priesthood and Christ

The consecration of Aaron and his sons was more than an ancient ceremony—it foreshadowed the eternal priesthood of Christ. The author of Hebrews draws the connection: "Every priest stands daily at his service, offering repeatedly the same sacrifices, which can never take away sins. But when Christ had offered for all time a single sacrifice for sins, he sat down at the right hand of God" (Heb. 10:11–12).

Where Aaron needed cleansing, Christ was sinless. Where Aaron stood daily, Christ sits in triumph. The Levitical priests could only point toward holiness; Jesus embodies it. Their ordination required the blood of bulls and rams; his required his own.

The anointing oil and priestly garments find their spiritual counterpart in the church. Peter declares that believers are now "a royal priesthood" (1 Pet. 2:9). Every Christian, cleansed by baptism and anointed by the Spirit, is called to serve in holiness. We offer not animal sacrifices but "spiritual sacrifices acceptable to God through Jesus Christ" (1 Pet. 2:5). Our ministry, like Aaron's, begins with cleansing, continues in obedience, and ends in fellowship.

In this way, Leviticus 8–10 bridges law and gospel. The same God who demanded holiness in the tabernacle now supplies it through his Son and extends it through his people.

The weight of holiness

These chapters press one truth into every reader's heart: holiness is beautiful but dangerous. The fire that consumed Nadab and Abihu was the same fire that consumed the burnt offering. God's presence is not safe—but it is good. He must be approached on his terms.

For those who serve in worship and leadership today, Leviticus 10 remains a sober mirror. Ministry is not performance; it is stewardship of the sacred. Whether preaching, singing, or serving, we stand in a holy place. Our calling demands both humility and precision. God is honored not by our creativity but by our conformity to his word.

Yet holiness is not meant to terrify believers but to draw them nearer. The priesthood of Christ transforms the fire of judgment into the flame of fellowship. The same presence that once consumed now cleanses. The God who said, "Among those who are near me I will be sanctified," has made a way for all to come near through his Son.

APPLICATION

1. Holiness begins with cleansing

Aaron and his sons could not serve until they were washed. The same is true for Christians. Before anyone can minister, they must first be purified by the blood of Christ. Service without cleansing is hypocrisy. God does not use the unwashed vessel; he transforms it first. Baptism, confession, and continual repentance prepare Christians to serve with clean hands and hearts. Holiness is not inherited or performed—it is received. Like Aaron's anointing oil, the Spirit marks us for service. When we forget this, ministry becomes self-driven instead of Spirit-led. Every day, we must return to that basin of grace and be made new.

2. Worship requires reverent obedience

Nadab and Abihu's tragedy warns us that zeal is no substitute for obedience. They brought fire God had not commanded, and it cost them their lives. The lesson remains vital: sincerity never replaces submission. In worship, we approach God on his terms, not our own. Whether offering praise, leading prayer, or breaking bread, the question is not "Do we like it?" but "Did God authorize it?" Reverence means respecting his word. When believers treat worship lightly or invent new patterns, they risk the same fate—displeasing the One they claim to honor. True worship is joyful obedience wrapped in awe.

3. God's servants must practice discernment

After the fire fell, God told Aaron that priests must stay sober "to distinguish between the holy and the common." Spiritual discernment is essential for anyone who leads or teaches. A clouded mind cannot guard holiness. In a world that blurs moral lines, believers must remain alert—clear in thought, grounded in Scripture, and guided by truth. This applies not only to literal sobriety but also to spiritual focus. Distraction, ambition, and pride dull the senses as surely as drink. Those set apart to serve must keep their judgment sharp, their motives pure, and their minds anchored in the word.

4. Christ transforms our service

Aaron stood trembling before the altar; Christ stands victorious at the right hand of God. His perfect priesthood changes everything. We no longer bring bulls or rams—we bring ourselves, consecrated by his blood. Every Christian is now part of that royal priesthood, called to intercede, to offer spiritual sacrifices, and to reflect his holiness in the world. Ministry is not limited to pulpits or communion tables; it happens wherever cleansed hands serve others. Because Christ is our High Priest, we serve confidently, knowing the fire that once consumed now refines. Holiness has become our calling, not our fear.

CONCLUSION

Leviticus 8–10 reminds believers that serving a holy God is both an honor and a hazard. Aaron's consecration showed that ministry begins with cleansing and calling, while Nadab and Abihu's death showed that holiness cannot be handled carelessly. Yet the story ends not in fear but in grace. Through Christ, the perfect High Priest, God has made every believer part of a royal priesthood—cleansed, anointed, and sent to serve. The same fire that once consumed now refines, empowering the church to reflect his glory in the world.

Next, Leviticus 11–12 will extend holiness beyond the tabernacle, showing how even daily life can honor the God who dwells among his people.

REFLECTION

1. Why was Aaron's consecration necessary before beginning priestly service?

2. What did the washing and anointing symbolize in the ordination ceremony?

3. How did the fire from the Lord show approval of Aaron's first offerings?

4. What was Nadab and Abihu's sin, and why was it so serious?

5. How did God's warning about wine teach discernment for priests?

6. How does Christ's perfect priesthood fulfill the role Aaron could only foreshadow?

DISCUSSION

1. What practices help you maintain personal holiness in daily service?

2. How can Christians balance zeal for God with careful obedience to his word?

3. What modern examples resemble "unauthorized fire" in worship or ministry?

4. How can we cultivate discernment to distinguish holy from common?

5. In what ways does Christ's priesthood transform our service and confidence?

6. How can the church today honor God's holiness without becoming legalistic?

4

HOLY BODIES, HOLY BIRTH

LEVITICUS 11–12

Objective: To understand how purity laws taught daily holiness and pointed to Christ's cleansing power.

INTRODUCTION

A friend once bought a used pickup from a rancher who had raised goats. The truck ran fine, but for months it carried the faint smell of livestock. No matter how many times he scrubbed the interior, the scent lingered—a reminder that what we touch leaves traces behind.

That simple truth lies at the heart of Leviticus 11–12. These chapters are not about superstition or hygiene; they teach how proximity shapes purity. What Israel touched, ate, and handled mattered because they lived in the presence of a holy God. Holiness wasn't confined to the tabernacle—it followed them to the dinner table, the marketplace, and the birthing room.

Through distinctions between clean and unclean, God taught his people to discern, to slow down, and to remember who they were. Even the joy and vulnerability of childbirth required cleansing, not because life was dirty, but because holiness is serious. Every law reminded Israel that the God who rescued them from Egypt wanted to dwell among them—and nothing unclean could stand in that presence.

EXAMINATION

A holy God and ordinary life (11:1-2)

Leviticus 11–12 shifts from the tabernacle to the table, from priests at the altar to families in their tents. After the intensity of sacrifices and ordination, these chapters answer a new question: how should ordinary Israelites live in the presence of a holy God? "Speak to the people of Israel, saying, These are the living things that you may eat…" (11:2).

Holiness in Israel was not confined to worship; it extended to eating, touching, and even childbirth. The message was simple but sweeping—God's people were to be distinct in every dimension of life. Nothing was too mundane to fall outside his concern. By defining what was clean and unclean, God taught Israel to discern between what is fitting for fellowship with him and what is not.

Clean and unclean animals (11:3-23)

The longest section of this unit classifies animals according to categories—land, sea, air, and crawling things. Clean animals could be eaten; unclean could not. The distinctions may seem arbitrary to modern readers, but each served a theological and pedagogical purpose.

Land Animals (11:3-8). Permitted animals were those that both chewed the cud and had a split hoof—such as cattle, sheep, and goats. Animals lacking one or both traits, like pigs or camels, were forbidden. The dual requirement instilled mindfulness: not everything common was permissible. Israel's diet would constantly remind them of divine order.

Sea Creatures (11:9-12). Fish with fins and scales were allowed; shellfish and other aquatic life were prohibited. Again, the rule was simple, memorable, and daily. Meals became moments of moral reflection.

Birds and Insects (11:13-23). Birds of prey and carrion eaters—vultures, owls, hawks—were unclean, likely because they fed on death. Winged insects were generally unclean except for certain locusts, crickets, and grasshoppers (11:21-22). The purpose was not arbitrary disgust but moral distinction: God's people were to avoid what symbolized corruption, predation, or decay.

While modern commentators have suggested hygienic motives, Leviticus emphasizes holiness, not health. These food laws created a visible boundary that separated Israel from surrounding nations. Every meal became an act of obedience, a reaffirmation that fellowship with God affects even appetite and choice. To eat according to God's word was to live as God's people.

Contact with death (11:24–47)

The chapter closes by addressing contamination through contact with carcasses. Anyone who touched the dead body of an unclean animal became unclean until evening and had to wash both body and clothes (11:24–28, 39–40). Even vessels and ovens could become defiled and had to be broken or purified (11:32–35). The meticulous detail underscores the seriousness of impurity.

Why such concern? Because death was the ultimate symbol of sin's curse. In Eden, death entered through disobedience; now every contact with decay reminded Israel of separation from life and holiness. These laws were not about germs but theology: God is the living One, and his people must shun the marks of mortality.

The closing verses (11:44–45) give the rationale: "For I am the Lord your God. Consecrate yourselves therefore, and be holy, for I am holy... For I am the Lord who brought you up out of the land of Egypt to be your God." Israel's dietary laws were not arbitrary restrictions but responses to redemption. Because God had redeemed them, they must reflect his character. Holiness was both identity and gratitude.

Purification after childbirth (12:1–8)

Chapter 12 narrows the lens from the community to the family, describing purification after childbirth. "If a woman conceives and bears a male child, she shall be unclean seven days... and on the eighth day the flesh of his foreskin shall be circumcised" (12:2–3).

The mother's impurity was not moral guilt but ritual defilement—symbolic of life's vulnerability and the transmission of mortality. Childbirth, while beautiful, brought a reminder of the fall: "In pain you shall bring forth children" (Gen. 3:16). Blood loss and contact with bodily fluids made the mother ceremonially unclean.

After the initial seven days, she remained in a period of purification for thirty-three days (12:4). During that time, she did not enter the sanctuary or touch holy things. If she bore a female child, the period doubled to eighty days (12:5). The text gives no explicit reason for the difference, though many scholars suggest it reinforced the seriousness of life-giving and the need for full recovery.

When the purification was complete, the woman brought a burnt offering and a sin offering—typically a lamb and a pigeon. If she could not afford a lamb, two birds sufficed. The priest then made atonement for her, and she was declared clean (12:6–8).

This ritual did not condemn motherhood; it sanctified it. The offerings celebrated life's restoration and acknowledged dependence on God for both conception and cleansing. The inclusion of the poor again reveals divine compassion—grace was accessible to all.

Luke records that Mary and Joseph followed this exact procedure after Jesus' birth, bringing "a pair of turtledoves or two young pigeons" (Luke 2:24). Even the mother of the Messiah submitted to the law's call for purification. The one born holy entered a world that needed cleansing.

The meaning of purity laws

Leviticus never explains its categories of clean and unclean in scientific terms. Their purpose was symbolic and covenantal. "Clean" signified wholeness, order, and alignment with creation's purpose; "unclean" represented disorder, decay, and separation. God was teaching his people to distinguish between what reflects his life-giving holiness and what reflects the corruption of sin.

Through repeated acts of discernment—choosing the right foods, avoiding carcasses, purifying after birth—Israel learned to think theologically about the physical world. Holiness was not abstract but embodied. Daily routines became rehearsals in obedience.

Moreover, these distinctions made Israel visibly distinct from its neighbors. Pagan worship often involved eating animals that were unclean or associating birth and fertility with idolatry. By rejecting those practices, Israel proclaimed allegiance to the true God. Holiness meant maintaining boundaries that mirrored God's own order in creation. To blur those boundaries was to blur the difference between Creator and creature.

Purity and the new covenant

When Jesus came, he honored the law's holiness while transforming its application. In Mark 7:18–19, he declared that nothing entering from outside can defile a person; "thus he declared all foods clean." Purity was no longer about diet but about the heart: "What comes out of a person is what defiles him."

Peter learned the same lesson in Acts 10, when a vision of unclean animals taught him that God's cleansing extended to Gentiles: "What God has made clean, do not call common." The gospel broke the ceremonial boundaries, revealing that holiness was no longer maintained by separation but by sanctification through the Spirit.

Yet the principle of Leviticus remains. Peter quotes its refrain directly: "You shall be holy, for I am holy" (1 Pet. 1:16). The call to discern, to remain pure, and to reflect God's character still governs Christian life—now inwardly rather than ritually. The difference is location: holiness has moved from the kitchen table to the human heart.

The purity laws pointed forward to Christ, the one who could touch the leper and remain undefiled, who entered death itself and emerged uncorrupted. In him, holiness becomes contagious rather than fragile.

Lessons in everyday holiness

Leviticus 11–12 teaches that God's holiness touches every sphere of life—what we eat, how we recover, even how we celebrate new birth. These laws reminded Israel daily that living in covenant with a holy God required awareness, gratitude, and self-restraint. Holiness was never meant to be confined to the tabernacle but woven through every act of existence.

For Christians, the same truth applies. The gospel frees us from ceremonial boundaries but not from moral vigilance. Whether eating, resting, or raising children, believers embody holiness through gratitude, moderation, and compassion. The ordinary becomes sacred when offered to God.

The childbirth laws in particular remind us that life's most human experiences—pain, recovery, and renewal—belong to God's domain. In Christ, even birth and blood point to redemption. Through his own suffering, new life is born for the world. The cycle of impurity and cleansing finds its final resolution in the cross, where death and defilement are conquered forever.

The call to be holy

Leviticus closes this section with a direct command: "You shall therefore separate the clean beast from the unclean... You shall be holy to me, for I the Lord am holy and have separated you from the peoples, that you should be mine" (Lev. 20:25-26).

Holiness means belonging. God's people are holy because they are his. The categories of Leviticus—clean and unclean, pure and defiled—were never arbitrary fences but symbols of that relationship. The Israelites learned daily that holiness was not self-made; it was conferred through covenant and maintained through obedience.

Today, holiness still means living distinctively, though not through diet or ritual. It means shaping our choices—our speech, habits, and desires—by the same principle that governed Israel's meals: if God dwells among us, everything we touch must reflect him.

APPLICATION

1. Holiness touches every part of life

Leviticus refuses to let holiness remain confined to the tabernacle. The same God who spoke from the Most Holy Place also spoke about what Israel could eat and how mothers should recover after childbirth. Every detail mattered because every part of life belonged to him. Christians often separate the sacred from the ordinary, treating Sunday worship as holy and weekday life as neutral. But holiness is not a compartment; it's a calling. Paul said, "Whether you eat or drink, or whatever you do, do all to the glory of God" (1 Cor. 10:31). How we work, speak, rest, and even eat should reveal that we belong to the God who redeemed us. The God of Leviticus still wants his people to reflect his purity in the small habits that fill every day.

2. Purity requires discernment

The laws of clean and unclean animals trained Israel's instincts. Before every meal, they had to pause and remember the difference between holy and common. That daily rhythm cultivated mindfulness—a spiritual reflex that asked, "Is this fitting for God's people?" Christians, though freed from dietary codes, still need disciplined discernment. The choices we make about what we read, watch, and support shape our hearts as surely as Israel's diet shaped theirs. Some things may not be sinful but still corrode holiness. Spiritual maturity means learning to separate what nourishes the soul from what defiles it. The Holy Spirit replaces the old categories of "clean" and "unclean" with a new command: "Whatever is pure… think about these things" (Phil. 4:8). Holiness grows through careful choices made with reverence and love for God.

3. Holiness does not despise the body

The laws concerning childbirth remind us that holiness and humanity are not opposites. The woman who bore a child was not condemned—she was honored through purification. God recognized the cost and fragility of life, and he cared for mothers in their vulnerability. In Christ, this truth deepens: our bodies are temples of the Holy Spirit (1 Cor. 6:19). Physical life is not a distraction from faith but its setting. Caring for health, practicing self-control, and honoring marital intimacy are acts of worship. Modern culture swings between worshiping the body and despising it; holiness charts a better way. We neither idolize nor ignore the body—we present it as a living sacrifice (Rom. 12:1). The God who sanctified childbirth still meets us in the flesh, teaching us to glorify him in strength and weakness alike.

4. Christ cleanses what we cannot

Israel's purity system exposed the problem it could never solve: uncleanness always returned. No matter how often they washed or sacrificed, the cycle continued. That repetition pointed forward to the one who would end it. Jesus touched lepers, ate with sinners, and entered death itself without becoming defiled. In him, holiness became contagious rather than fragile. His blood cleanses not just hands but consciences (Heb. 9:14). Christians no longer fear contamination; we live from cleansing. Grace doesn't remove the call to holiness—it makes it possible. The Spirit now purifies what the law could only diagnose. Every believer can echo David's prayer, "Wash me, and I shall be whiter than snow" (Psa. 51:7). The God who once warned, "Do not touch," now says through Christ, "Be clean." Holiness has become a gift of grace and a life to pursue.

CONCLUSION

Leviticus 11–12 reminds us that holiness is not an event but a lifestyle. Israel learned that even the most ordinary activities—eating, working, giving birth—took place before the face of a holy God. Every boundary, every washing, every distinction between clean and unclean whispered the same truth: God's people must reflect God's purity.

In Christ, the shadow gives way to light. He touched what was unclean and made it clean; he entered death and turned it into life. Now holiness flows outward from the heart, transforming every task into worship.

Next, Leviticus 13–15 will continue this theme, showing how God's holiness confronts impurity and provides cleansing for what seems incurable.

REFLECTION

1. Why did God give Israel laws about clean and unclean animals?
2. How did contact with death symbolize sin's defilement in Leviticus 11?
3. What did the purification after childbirth teach about life and holiness?
4. How did Israel's diet reflect their covenant identity?
5. How do Jesus' words in Mark 7 fulfill Leviticus' purity principles?
6. What does "You shall be holy, for I am holy" mean in this context?

DISCUSSION

1. How can holiness shape your daily habits and routines?
2. What modern practices require discernment to stay spiritually clean?
3. How can Christians honor God through care of their bodies?
4. What does Christ's cleansing teach us about grace and responsibility?
5. In what ways can ordinary tasks become acts of holiness?
6. How does understanding Leviticus 11–12 deepen your appreciation for Jesus' ministry?

5

CONTAGIOUS DEFILEMENT
LEVITICUS 13–15

Objective: To understand how impurity spreads and how God's holiness restores through cleansing and grace.

INTRODUCTION

A few winters ago, a small patch of mold appeared in the corner of a kitchen wall. At first it seemed harmless—a minor stain easily ignored. But within weeks, it spread behind the cabinets, darkening the drywall and filling the air with a musty smell. By the time the homeowners investigated, the damage was deep and costly. What began as a spot had quietly taken over the room.

That's the image behind Leviticus 13–15. These chapters aren't about modern medicine but moral vision. God used physical impurity—skin disease, mildew, and bodily discharges—to teach his people how corruption spreads and how holiness must confront it. Just as mold grows in silence, sin thrives when left unchecked. The priest's careful inspection, the isolation, and the cleansing rituals all pointed to one truth: holiness must guard the camp.

Yet the story does not end with exclusion—it ends with restoration. The same God who declared the leper "unclean" also provided a path for healing. Leviticus reminds us that while defilement is contagious, grace is stronger still.

EXAMINATION

Holiness in a world of decay (13:1-2)

Few sections of Leviticus are as foreign to modern readers as chapters 13–15. Here, the focus moves from sacrifices and food to skin diseases, mildew, and bodily discharges. The language is technical, even uncomfortable, yet the message behind these laws is profound: holiness must confront the realities of human decay.

"The Lord spoke to Moses and Aaron, saying, 'When a person has on the skin of his body a swelling or an eruption or a spot… he shall be brought to Aaron the priest'" (Lev. 13:1-2). In Israel, illness was not only a physical issue but a spiritual one. Disease represented the presence of death—the very opposite of the life and wholeness found in God. If sin is the root of death, then decay, infection, and impurity are its symptoms in the world.

The laws of Leviticus 13-15 did not condemn the sick as sinners but taught Israel to recognize that human frailty could not coexist unguarded with divine holiness. Holiness demands separation until cleansing occurs. These chapters are not about quarantine alone—they are about theology lived out in community.

Diagnosing defilement: Skin diseases (13:1-46)

The priest's role in these chapters was not that of a physician but a spiritual examiner. His task was to discern whether a person's condition rendered them "clean" or "unclean." The Hebrew term often translated "leprosy" (*sara'at*) covered a range of skin disorders—white patches, raw flesh, swelling, or scabs. Modern readers should not think exclusively of modern Hansen's disease; the focus is ritual impurity, not medical classification.

The process was deliberate. The priest examined the infected area for depth, color, and spread (13:3-8). If uncertain, the person was isolated for seven days, then reexamined. Holiness demanded caution, not haste. The priest's decision determined one's ability to remain within the camp. If declared unclean, the individual lived "outside the camp," crying out, "Unclean, unclean," and dwelling alone (13:45-46).

This may seem cruel, yet the purpose was protective. Israel was a holy nation; the camp was the place where God's presence dwelled. Just as disease spreads through touch, so impurity spreads through unguarded contact. Isolation served both as a quarantine and as a symbol of how sin separates humanity from God and others.

The afflicted person's torn clothes and unkempt hair mirrored mourning customs—an outward confession of inward loss. They were not outcasts in the sense of punishment but living parables of the damage sin brings into the world. The priest's careful inspection reminded the nation that holiness is not indifferent to corruption.

The defilement of fabrics and houses (13:47–59; 14:33–57)

Surprisingly, the same Hebrew term *saraʿat* also described mold or mildew in garments and houses. God's holiness extended beyond the human body to the spaces where people lived. If discoloration appeared on cloth or leather, the priest examined it; if it spread, the material was burned (13:52). If contained, it was washed and quarantined.

Later, when Israel entered Canaan, the same principle applied to houses (14:33–48). If green or reddish spots appeared on the walls, stones were removed, and the structure was scraped and replastered. Persistent contamination required demolition. These procedures, though practical, were primarily theological—they dramatized God's refusal to dwell amid corruption.

The message was unmistakable: impurity infects everything it touches. What begins as a blemish can spread through an entire home. Sin operates the same way—quiet, invasive, and destructive. The only solution is cleansing and renewal, not denial. The priestly inspection of walls and fabrics anticipated the work of God's Spirit, who examines hearts and exposes hidden decay.

The restoration ritual for a healed house (14:48–53) echoed the purification of a healed person: two birds were used, one slain and one released, signifying both atonement and freedom. The same pattern of grace applied to all creation—life restored through substitution.

The cleansing of the healed (14:1–32)

When a person was healed of skin disease, the priest conducted a detailed ritual of restoration. This two-stage process emphasized both purification and reintegration.

First, the priest met the healed person outside the camp and used two birds: one killed over running water, and the other dipped in the blood and released into the open field (14:4-7). This imagery symbolized life emerging from death—a powerful picture of renewal. The individual then washed, shaved, and reentered the camp but remained outside the tent for seven days.

On the eighth day, full restoration occurred through sacrifice: a guilt offering, sin offering, burnt offering, and grain offering (14:10-20). These offerings proclaimed gratitude and reaffirmed fellowship with God. For the poor, alternate sacrifices were provided, once again showing that grace was not limited by wealth (14:21-32).

The ritual's climax came when the priest placed blood and oil on the person's right ear, thumb, and big toe—the same actions used in the priests' ordination (8:23-24). In other words, the cleansed person was reconsecrated to God's service. Their restoration was not merely physical but spiritual. To be healed was to be set apart again for holiness.

Discharges and bodily impurity (15:1-33)

Chapter 15 addresses discharges from the body—male and female, natural and abnormal. The details are explicit because the theology is serious: life and death flow through the body, and any loss of life-bearing fluid symbolized the intrusion of death.

A man with a chronic discharge (15:2-12) rendered himself and anything he touched unclean. Even objects like saddles or beds required washing. When the discharge ceased, the man waited seven days, bathed, and offered sacrifices for cleansing (15:13-15). Similarly, seminal emission caused temporary impurity requiring washing until evening (15:16-18).

For women, menstruation produced uncleanness for seven days; anyone who touched her or her bedding shared her condition (15:19-24). Extended bleeding—like that of the woman healed by Jesus in Mark 5—required additional purification (15:25-30). These laws did not shame natural functions; they acknowledged human frailty in the presence of divine perfection. God was teaching Israel that holiness and life are inseparable. Whenever life ebbed, ritual cleansing reminded them of dependence on his sustaining power.

The chapter ends with a summary that ties all the preceding material together: "Thus you shall keep the people of Israel separate from their uncleanness, lest they die in their uncleanness by defiling my tabernacle that is in their midst" (15:31).

Holiness protected life; impurity endangered it. The tabernacle was not a symbol of exclusion but a sanctuary of life—defilement could not coexist there.

Theology of impurity: Sin and separation

Why did God care so much about mildew, sores, and discharges? Because each represented the intrusion of death into a world meant for life. In the Garden of Eden, death entered through sin, and ever since, every trace of decay has borne witness to that fall. Leviticus 13–15 is not about hygiene—it is about hope. It acknowledges the world's brokenness while affirming that cleansing is possible.

Uncleanness was not the same as sin, but it pointed to sin's consequences. A skin disease was not a moral failure, yet it illustrated what sin does: it isolates, spreads, and corrupts. The leper outside the camp mirrored the sinner cut off from God. The only path back was through priestly mediation, cleansing, and sacrifice.

These chapters train believers to view holiness not as moral perfectionism but as restored fellowship. God's holiness is not fragile—it is powerful. He does not withdraw from impurity; he conquers it through cleansing.

The fulfillment in Christ: Touching the untouchable

In the Gospels, Jesus repeatedly fulfills the imagery of Leviticus 13–15. When a man "full of leprosy" approached him, saying, "Lord, if you will, you can make me clean," Jesus did the unthinkable—he touched him (Luke 5:12–13). Under the law, that act should have rendered Jesus unclean, but instead, purity flowed outward. "Immediately the leprosy left him."

The same pattern appears with the woman suffering chronic bleeding (Mark 5:25–34). For twelve years she had been excluded, untouchable, and isolated. Yet when she reached out and touched Jesus' garment, she was instantly healed. In both stories, holiness triumphed over impurity. The power of God in Christ reversed the direction of defilement.

In doing so, Jesus demonstrated that the holiness symbolized in Leviticus had come in person. He is both priest and sacrifice, the one who examines, heals, and restores. Where the old law required separation, the gospel announces reconciliation. The leper no longer cries "Unclean!" but proclaims the mercy of God.

The church now carries forward that ministry of cleansing—not through ritual but through compassion, truth, and the gospel. When Christians reach out to the broken and the marginalized, they reenact the same holiness that touched the leper's skin. Holiness is not isolation from sinners; it is restoration through grace.

The hope of cleansing

Leviticus 13–15 ends where the gospel begins—with the possibility of renewal. No corruption is too deep, no impurity too stubborn, for God's holiness to overcome. The priest who inspected sores and stains pointed to the greater Priest who inspects hearts and heals what is hidden.

In a world where moral and physical decay still spread like mold in a wall, the message remains: holiness is contagious when it comes from God. The same God who told Israel to guard against defilement now calls his people to spread purity through service, mercy, and truth.

The one who cleansed lepers still cleanses consciences. He removes shame, restores community, and fills his house with life. Every stain of sin, every scar of brokenness, can be washed away in his grace.

APPLICATION

1. Sin spreads like disease

The laws of skin disease remind us that sin is never contained. Like an infection, it begins small but soon spreads through thoughts, habits, and relationships. What starts as a private compromise can poison an entire home or congregation. Israel's quarantine laws were God's way of teaching his people that corruption cannot be ignored—it must be confronted. Paul used the same image when he warned, "a little leaven leavens the whole lump" (1 Cor. 5:6). Holiness demands vigilance. The call to confession and repentance is not about shame but prevention. When Christians take sin seriously and seek cleansing quickly, they protect the health of the whole body. Avoiding spiritual infection begins with humble honesty before God and one another.

2. God's holiness extends to every corner of life

Mildew in fabric and mold in walls may seem trivial, but God used them to show that holiness belongs in every corner of life. The priest who examined a home was teaching Israel that God's concern doesn't end at the sanctuary door. He wants purity in how we live, work, and dwell. Modern Christians face the same challenge: does holiness shape our homes, our language, and our attitudes? The God who inspected Israel's tents still walks among his people, seeking sincerity and integrity. Our homes are not neutral spaces—they are extensions of worship. A clean house in Leviticus was a symbol of renewed fellowship; a holy household today becomes a living temple where God's presence abides.

3. Christ restores what sin has ruined

Every ritual of cleansing in Leviticus pointed forward to Christ's compassion. He touched the leper, healed the outcast, and entered death to bring life. The people others avoided were the ones he restored. His holiness was not fragile—it was contagious. The cross became the ultimate purification ritual, where defilement met divine mercy. Christians who have been cleansed by that grace are now called to extend it. We touch the untouchable through acts of kindness, forgiveness, and service. The world still bears the marks of decay—addiction, bitterness, guilt—but Christ's people carry the healing power of his presence. Holiness today is not withdrawal from the unclean but redemptive contact that reflects the heart of our Savior.

4. Cleansing must lead to community

When a leper was healed, the priest declared him clean and restored him to the camp. Cleansing always led to community. God's goal was never isolation for its own sake but restoration to fellowship. The same principle governs the church. Forgiveness through Christ reconciles believers not only to God but also to one another. The one who was once "outside the camp" now belongs to the family of faith. This truth challenges Christians to build communities of grace where no one remains excluded by shame. When we welcome the repentant and bear one another's burdens, we demonstrate that holiness and mercy are not opposites—they are partners. A pure church is not a gated community but a family of restored sinners gathered around grace.

CONCLUSION

Leviticus 13–15 confronts the uncomfortable truth that impurity spreads faster than we imagine. What begins as a blemish or stain can quickly corrupt what is holy. Yet the same God who commanded separation also offered restoration. Every inspection, washing, and sacrifice pointed to his desire not to cast out but to cleanse. Through Christ, holiness has become redemptive rather than restrictive—the touch that once defiled now heals.

The leper's cry, "Unclean, unclean," has been silenced by the Savior's words, "Be clean." His holiness still calls us to vigilance, but also to compassion for the broken.

Next, Leviticus 16 will reach the center of the book and the heart of atonement—the Day of Atonement itself.

REFLECTION

1. Why did priests, not physicians, diagnose impurity in Israel?
2. What did isolation from the camp teach about holiness and sin?
3. How did God's laws about houses and garments teach moral lessons?
4. What message did the two birds in the cleansing ritual symbolize?
5. How do Leviticus' purity laws reveal the seriousness of defilement?
6. How does Jesus' healing of lepers fulfill these chapters' meaning?

DISCUSSION

1. What examples show how sin spreads quietly in our lives or churches?
2. How can we invite God's holiness into our homes and routines?
3. What does Christ's willingness to touch the unclean teach us today?
4. How can the church reflect both holiness and compassion?
5. Why is community restoration essential after forgiveness?
6. How can we guard against spiritual "contamination" without becoming isolating or proud?

6

THE DAY OF ATONEMENT
LEVITICUS 16

Objective: To understand how the Day of Atonement foreshadows Christ's perfect, once-for-all sacrifice for sin.

INTRODUCTION

In 1874, workers cleaning the ceiling of a grand cathedral discovered that centuries of candle soot had turned the stone nearly black. For generations, worshipers had prayed beneath what they thought was dark rock—until the cleaning revealed bright white marble beneath. The grime had built up slowly, almost invisibly, until no one remembered what purity looked like.

Leviticus 16 addresses the same problem on a spiritual scale. Sin accumulates—quietly, persistently—until the soul forgets its need for cleansing. The Day of Atonement was God's annual act of restoration, the moment when the nation's guilt was acknowledged, covered, and removed. The high priest entered the Holy of Holies with blood, not words, to reconcile a sinful people to a holy God.

Every detail of this solemn day pointed beyond itself—to a future Priest who would enter once for all, not into an earthly tent but into heaven itself. Leviticus 16 reminds us that forgiveness is costly, holiness is beautiful, and grace is never cheap. The blood that cleansed the sanctuary then is the same blood that cleanses hearts today.

EXAMINATION

The holy of holies and the weight of sin (16:1–2)

Leviticus 16 stands at the center of the book and the heart of Israel's worship. Everything before it prepared for this day; everything after it flows from it. The opening verse sets the tone: "The Lord spoke to Moses after the death of the two sons of Aaron, when they drew near before the Lord and died" (16:1). Nadab and Abihu's disobedience still hung over Israel as a warning. No one approached God casually.

Once a year, and only once, the high priest entered the Most Holy Place to make atonement for the nation. Every other day of the year, access was barred—"tell Aaron your brother not to come at any time into the Holy Place inside the veil, before the mercy seat… that he may not die" (16:2). God's presence was both promise and peril. Holiness invited fellowship but demanded reverence.

The Day of Atonement (*Yom Kippur*) was the most solemn day on Israel's calendar. It addressed not only individual sins but the accumulated defilement of the entire nation. Through a series of sacrifices and rituals, God provided cleansing for the sanctuary, the priests, and the people, reestablishing the relationship that sin had strained.

The high priest's preparation (16:3–6)

Before Aaron could make atonement for others, he had to be cleansed himself. "But in this way Aaron shall come into the Holy Place: with a bull from the herd for a sin offering and a ram for a burnt offering" (16:3). Even the high priest, clothed with sacred garments, needed forgiveness.

On this day he did not wear the ornate vestments described in Exodus 28—the ephod, breastpiece, and golden turban—but simple linen garments (16:4). The humility of his attire reflected the gravity of the moment. The mediator between God and Israel entered as a servant, not a spectacle. He washed his body, symbolizing purity, and offered the bull as a sin offering for himself and his household (16:6). Only after his own sins were addressed could he act on behalf of others.

This ritual humility pointed forward to Christ, who "emptied himself, taking the form of a servant" (Phil. 2:7). The priest who dared not enter without blood prefigured the Savior who entered heaven itself with his own blood, perfect and unblemished.

The two goats: substitution and removal (16:7–10)

The heart of the ceremony involved two goats. Aaron cast lots—one "for the Lord" and the other "for Azazel" (16:8). The first goat was slain as a sin offering; its blood was sprinkled within the veil. The second, the scapegoat, was sent alive into the wilderness, carrying away the people's sins.

Scholars debate the meaning of "Azazel," but the symbolism is clear: sin must be both atoned for and removed. The first goat satisfied divine justice; the second dramatized divine mercy. Together they portray the fullness of forgiveness—one life given, one burden lifted.

After killing the goat for the Lord, Aaron entered the Most Holy Place with its blood and sprinkled it on and before the mercy seat (16:15). The term "mercy seat" (*kapporet*) means "place of atonement." Blood on the mercy seat signified that life had been given in place of death. The law within the ark condemned the people, but the blood above it declared mercy.

The scapegoat ritual followed. Aaron placed both hands on its head, confessing "all the iniquities of the people of Israel, and all their transgressions, all their sins" (16:21). The repetition—iniquities, transgressions, sins—underscored completeness. Every category of guilt was transferred symbolically to the animal, which was then led into the wilderness "to a remote area." There, it bore the sins of the people, never to return.

The people watched as their guilt disappeared into the distance. The ritual expressed visually what Psalm 103:12 would later declare: "As far as the east is from the west, so far does he remove our transgressions from us."

Cleansing the sanctuary (16:11–19)

The Day of Atonement addressed a problem most Israelites never saw: the defilement of the sanctuary itself. Even holy spaces could become polluted by human sin. The blood of the sin offerings cleansed the tabernacle because the sins of the people had symbolically accumulated there throughout the year. "Thus he shall make atonement for the Holy Place, because of the uncleannesses of the people of Israel and because of their transgressions" (16:16).

This was a profound truth—sin not only corrupts individuals but contaminates the very environment of worship. God's dwelling must be purified if fellowship is to continue. The sprinkling of blood reconsecrated the sacred space, reaffirming that life conquers death and holiness conquers impurity.

The priest applied blood to the altar seven times (16:19), the number of completeness. Through these actions, Israel's relationship with God was symbolically reset. The covenant bond was renewed for another year.

For Christians, this ritual offers both comfort and challenge. Sin still defiles worship, though not through ritual pollution but through the heart. True cleansing requires more than external blood—it requires inward renewal through the Spirit (Heb. 9:13–14).

The people's humility (16:29–31)

While Aaron performed the rituals, the people participated through repentance. "It shall be a statute to you forever that in the seventh month… you shall afflict yourselves and shall do no work" (16:29). "Afflict yourselves" meant fasting and humbling the heart before God. Atonement was not a spectator event; it demanded contrition.

This was Israel's annual reset—a reminder that holiness could not be maintained without grace. On that day, all other work stopped. Sin was the nation's business; cleansing was God's work alone.

The purpose was not despair but renewal: "On this day shall atonement be made for you to cleanse you. You shall be clean before the Lord from all your sins" (16:30). No other day in the year carried such a promise. The Day of Atonement was both solemn and joyful—the nation's deepest repentance met God's greatest mercy.

Atonement: Substitution and satisfaction

Every act in Leviticus 16 reveals two dimensions of atonement—substitution and satisfaction. The slain goat satisfied the justice of God; the scapegoat substituted itself for the guilty and removed their shame. Atonement was not an abstract idea but a visible exchange: the innocent dies so the guilty may live.

The Hebrew word kippur (*atonement*) means "to cover." Blood covered what law exposed. Yet that covering was temporary. Each year the high priest repeated the same rituals, and each year sin's stain returned. The law revealed sin but could not erase it permanently.

The repetition itself preached a message: humanity needs a better priest and a better sacrifice. The shadow of Leviticus awaited its fulfillment in the light of Christ.

Fulfillment in Christ (Heb. 9–10)

The writer of Hebrews draws directly from Leviticus 16 to explain Jesus' work. "When Christ appeared as a high priest of the good things that have come... he entered once for all into the holy places, not by means of the blood of goats and calves but by means of his own blood, thus securing an eternal redemption" (Heb. 9:11–12). In Christ, every symbol of the Day of Atonement finds its reality:

- The veil separating humanity from God was torn (Matt. 27:51).
- The priest who entered trembling was replaced by a sinless mediator.
- The blood of animals was replaced by the blood of the Son.
- The scapegoat found its fulfillment when Jesus "suffered outside the gate" to sanctify the people (Heb. 13:12).

Unlike Aaron, Jesus did not need to cleanse himself before entering. His offering was final—"once for all" (Heb. 10:10). The high priest entered yearly; Christ entered eternally. The law reminded of guilt; the gospel removes it forever.

Through his death and resurrection, Christ achieved what Leviticus 16 anticipated: sin covered, guilt removed, and access restored. The atonement is no longer an annual event but a finished reality. Every believer now enters the presence of God without fear, "by the new and living way that he opened for us through the curtain" (Heb. 10:20).

The meaning for God's people today

The Day of Atonement teaches modern believers that holiness and mercy are not opposites but partners. God's holiness requires judgment, yet his mercy provides the substitute. The cross reveals both truths perfectly. Sin is serious enough to demand blood, but love is deep enough to provide it.

The annual rhythm of atonement has been replaced by continual access. We no longer wait for a high priest to emerge from the veil; we have a high priest seated at the right hand of God. Yet the call to humility remains. Just as Israel "afflicted their souls," Christians confess their sins and approach the throne of grace with reverence.

The Day of Atonement also reminds the church of its mission. The scapegoat carried sin into the wilderness so that the camp could remain pure. The church, too, bears witness to the world that sin must be carried away—not hidden or excused. We proclaim that in Christ, guilt is not ignored but transferred and forgiven.

The holiness of access

Leviticus 16 reveals both the danger and the privilege of approaching God. Aaron could enter the Holy of Holies only with blood, only once a year, and only as God commanded. Today, believers have continual access through Christ's intercession, yet that access must never breed casualness. "Therefore let us be grateful for receiving a kingdom that cannot be shaken, and thus let us offer to God acceptable worship, with reverence and awe" (Heb. 12:28).

Holiness has not been diluted by grace; it has been deepened. The presence that once burned with danger now welcomes with love—but it is still holy ground. The mercy seat has become a throne of grace, but the same God sits upon it.

APPLICATION

1. We approach God only through the blood of Christ

The high priest could enter the Holy of Holies only with blood, a solemn reminder that access to God requires atonement. Modern believers enjoy direct fellowship with God, but that privilege was purchased at a terrible cost—the blood of Jesus. We must never confuse freedom with familiarity. Every prayer, every song, every act of worship passes through the merit of Christ's sacrifice. When we gather at the Lord's table, we stand where Aaron stood—before the mercy seat. Our confidence is not in ourselves but in the cross. The Day of Atonement teaches that grace is costly and that the way into God's presence remains open only because the perfect High Priest still intercedes for his people.

2. Sin demands both confession and cleansing

Two goats—one slain, one released—teach that forgiveness involves more than pardon; it includes purification. The slain goat covered guilt before God, and the scapegoat carried shame away from the people. In Christ, both are complete. Yet Christians must still confess, naming sins instead of hiding them. Confession is not groveling—it's agreeing with God about the truth. When we refuse to confess, we keep our sins in the camp; when we confess, Christ bears them away. True repentance isn't a ritual of words but a cleansing of heart and conscience. The Day of Atonement invites us to lay everything upon the Savior, confident that he removes sin "as far as the east is from the west" (Psa. 103:12).

3. Holiness requires humility and rest

On the Day of Atonement, Israel was commanded to "afflict their souls" and do no work. Forgiveness came not by effort but by grace. The people stood still while the priest worked on their behalf. That same principle defines the gospel: salvation is God's doing, not ours. Christians often strive to earn approval through performance, forgetting that atonement is already finished. Holiness begins with humility—a willingness to rest in what Christ has done. Yet this rest is not passivity; it's trust that leads to obedience. When we stop working to prove ourselves, we begin living to please God. The Day of Atonement whispers through the ages: stop striving, and let grace do its work.

4. God's mercy is meant to renew his people

The Day of Atonement reset Israel's relationship with God each year, cleansing the sanctuary and the nation. It was a new beginning—a chance to start clean. For Christians, that renewal is constant. Every time we remember the cross, confess our sins, or partake of communion, we relive the joy of restored fellowship. God's mercy is not a one-time pardon but a lifelong power to renew. Just as the high priest emerged from the veil to bless the people, our risen Savior intercedes continually for us. The assurance of cleansing should move us to gratitude and holy living. Atonement is not an excuse to sin more but a reason to love more deeply. The mercy seat has become our meeting place with God, where grace renews us every day.

CONCLUSION

Leviticus 16 reaches the mountaintop of the book—and the shadow of the cross. Once a year, Israel watched its high priest disappear behind the veil, bearing blood for the nation. When he returned, forgiveness and relief filled the camp. But when Christ entered the true Holy of Holies, he never came back in the same way. His work was finished, his offering complete, his blood eternal. The torn veil now invites every believer into the presence of God.

The Day of Atonement reveals what Calvary accomplished and what communion celebrates: sin removed, access granted, and holiness restored.

Next, Leviticus 17–20 will unfold the practical outworking of that holiness in daily life—the call to live with God in purity, justice, and love.

REFLECTION

1. Why could the high priest enter the Holy of Holies only once a year?
2. What did the two goats together symbolize about forgiveness?
3. Why was the sanctuary itself cleansed on the Day of Atonement?
4. How did the people participate while the priest made atonement?
5. What key word or action summarized the purpose of the entire ritual?
6. How does Hebrews describe Christ as the ultimate fulfillment of this day?

DISCUSSION

1. How should Christ's sacrifice shape the way we approach God in worship?
2. What can the two goats teach us about confession and forgiveness?
3. In what ways do believers still "afflict their souls" before God today?
4. How can resting in grace free us from self-reliance and guilt?
5. Why should atonement lead to renewal rather than complacency?
6. How can the church reflect God's mercy toward those seeking a new beginning?

7

THE HOLINESS CODE
LEVITICUS 17–20

Objective: To understand how holiness shapes every part of life and reflects belonging to a holy God.

INTRODUCTION

In a museum in Florence hangs Michelangelo's unfinished statue known as *The Awakening Slave*. The figure appears to be straining to free itself from the marble block, its form emerging but not yet complete. The sculptor began with something ordinary—stone—and sought to reveal something extraordinary within.

That image captures the purpose of Leviticus 17–20. God was shaping a people who would reflect his holiness in a world of corruption. These chapters—often called the holiness code—move from the altar to the home, from sacrifice to sexuality, from worship to work. They reveal that holiness is not a priestly privilege but a calling for God's chosen people.

Israel was to be distinct not because they were better, but because they belonged. The same God who redeemed them from Egypt wanted to carve his character into their lives—mercy, integrity, justice, and purity. Holiness was not isolation from the world; it was transformation within it.

Through these commands, God taught Israel—and still teaches his church—that holiness touches every thought, word, and relationship. The chisel of obedience shapes the heart into the likeness of its Creator.

EXAMINATION

Holiness in every sphere of life (17:1-2)

Leviticus 17-20 forms what scholars call the holiness code—a collection of laws that show what it means to live as God's covenant people in every dimension of life. If Leviticus 1-16 taught Israel how to draw near to God through sacrifice and cleansing, these chapters teach how to stay near through obedience and moral integrity.

The section begins with a command: "Speak to Aaron and his sons and to all the people of Israel and say to them, This is the thing that the Lord has commanded" (17:2). Every person, priest or commoner, must live under the same divine authority. Holiness was not reserved for the sanctuary; it was the daily calling of everyone who bore God's name.

This "code" weaves worship, ethics, and compassion into a single fabric. It teaches that holiness is not isolation from the world but imitation of God. "You shall be holy, for I the Lord your God am holy" (19:2) serves as the refrain for the entire section.

The sacredness of blood (17:3-16)

The first command deals with the sanctity of sacrifice and the meaning of blood. Israel was forbidden to offer sacrifices anywhere except at the tabernacle (17:3-9). Any person who killed an animal for sacrifice in another place "shall be cut off from his people." This law preserved both unity and purity in worship. To sacrifice elsewhere was to invite idolatry.

Verse 11 gives the central theological statement: "For the life of the flesh is in the blood, and I have given it for you on the altar to make atonement for your souls, for it is the blood that makes atonement by the life."

Blood was not magical—it was sacred because it represented life, which belongs to God alone. By forbidding the eating or misuse of blood (17:10-14), God taught Israel to revere life as his gift and atonement as his grace. Every drop of blood reminded them that life and holiness are sustained only by divine mercy.

This principle reaches its climax in Christ, whose blood was "poured out for many for the forgiveness of sins" (Matt. 26:28). The blood that once cried from the altar now speaks from the cross (Heb. 12:24), testifying that life conquers death.

Moral and sexual holiness (18:1-30)

Chapter 18 moves from the sacredness of blood to the sacredness of relationships. God commanded Israel not to imitate the practices of Egypt or Canaan, "for by all these the nations I am driving out before you have become unclean" (18:24). The pagan world blurred moral boundaries; Israel had to reflect God's order.

The chapter details prohibitions against incest, adultery, homosexuality, and bestiality—acts that desecrate the covenant of marriage and the dignity of creation. While modern culture may recoil at these restrictions, their purpose is not repression but protection. Sexual sin was not merely private—it defiled the land itself, poisoning community life and provoking divine judgment (18:27-28).

God's design for sexuality reflects his holiness: exclusive, faithful, and life-giving. Every distortion—whether casual infidelity or idolatrous ritual—rejects his image. "You shall therefore keep my statutes and my rules; if a person does them, he shall live by them" (18:5). Obedience was the path to life, not limitation.

For Christians, these commands echo in Paul's writings: "This is the will of God, your sanctification: that you abstain from sexual immorality" (1 Thess. 4:3). Holiness is not a cultural artifact but an eternal reflection of God's character.

Holiness in community: justice and compassion (19:1-37)

Leviticus 19 is one of the richest ethical chapters in Scripture. It begins with the familiar refrain, "You shall be holy, for I the Lord your God am holy" (19:2), and then shows what holiness looks like in everyday behavior. The commandments move seamlessly between worship, morality, and social justice.

Worship and Reverence (19:3-8). Israel had to honor parents, keep the Sabbath, and reject idols. Family and worship were twin pillars of faithfulness. Reverence for God began with reverence for the structures he created.

Compassion and Integrity (19:9-18). Holiness extended to how Israelites treated the poor and the vulnerable. Farmers were to leave the edges of their fields for gleaners (19:9–10), a law later embodied in the story of Ruth. Honesty in business, fairness in judgment, and respect for the disabled and elderly all reflected God's compassion.

The heart of the chapter beats in verse 18: "You shall love your neighbor as yourself: I am the Lord." Jesus would later call this the second greatest commandment (Matt. 22:39). Love, in Leviticus, is not sentiment but justice lived out in daily faithfulness.

Purity and distinction (19:19–37)

The final section of the chapter reinforces the theme of distinction—no mixed breeding, mixed fabrics, or mixed loyalties. These tangible boundaries symbolized Israel's moral distinctiveness. God was training his people to live with integrity—to be whole in a world of compromise.

The closing verse summarizes the motive: "You shall observe all my statutes and all my rules, and do them: I am the Lord" (19:37). Holiness flows from identity. They obeyed not to become God's people but because they already were.

Holiness and accountability (Lev. 20:1–27)

Chapter 20 reinforces the previous laws by listing the consequences of disobedience. The penalties were severe because holiness was serious. Worshiping Molech, engaging in occult practices, and sexual perversions brought death or exile. "You shall be holy to me, for I the Lord am holy and have separated you from the peoples, that you should be mine" (20:26).

This separation was not arrogance but preservation. Israel's moral integrity was essential to its mission. The holiness code was God's way of creating a nation that would reflect his justice to the world. Sin was contagious, and the community had to guard against it.

Modern readers may struggle with these penalties, but they reveal divine compassion. A holy nation could not survive if it treated evil lightly. By establishing moral boundaries, God protected the covenant community from self-destruction.

The contrast between chapters 18 and 20—sin and its punishment—frames chapter 19's call to love and justice. Together, they show that holiness is both moral clarity and merciful compassion.

The pattern of holiness

Across these chapters, a pattern emerges: holiness is comprehensive. It sanctifies worship (ch. 17), sexuality (ch. 18), society (ch. 19), and justice (ch. 20). God does not divide life into sacred and secular. To belong to him is to bring every decision under his lordship.

The holiness code reveals the integrated nature of righteousness. You cannot honor God at the altar and exploit your neighbor in the marketplace. Holiness that ignores mercy or ethics is hypocrisy. Israel's obedience was to demonstrate the beauty of God's character to the watching nations. "Keep them and do them," Moses said elsewhere, "for that will be your wisdom and your understanding in the sight of the peoples" (Deut. 4:6).

The world still needs to see that kind of holiness—a faith that worships sincerely, loves deeply, and lives justly.

Fulfillment in Christ (1 Pet. 1:13–19)

The holiness code reaches its fulfillment in Christ, who embodies the holiness God demanded and now imparts it to his people. Peter quotes directly from Leviticus: "As he who called you is holy, you also be holy in all your conduct" (1 Pet. 1:15–16). Holiness is no longer maintained through ritual distinctions but through transformed hearts.

Jesus fulfilled the sacredness of blood through his own sacrifice; he fulfilled moral purity by resisting temptation; he fulfilled social justice by showing mercy to the poor and truth to the powerful. In him, holiness becomes relational rather than ritual.

Through the Spirit, Christians are empowered to live out the very ethics Leviticus describes. We care for the poor, honor marriage, tell the truth, and show compassion because we reflect the God who redeemed us. Grace does not erase the holiness code—it writes it on our hearts.

The church, then, is the new covenant community called to embody the same refrain: "You shall be holy, for I am holy." We do not fear defilement from the world; we bring holiness into it. The blood that once stayed inside the tabernacle now flows through the lives of those who belong to Christ.

The beauty of holiness

Leviticus 17–20 may seem demanding, but behind every command stands love. God called Israel to be different, not to restrict them but to protect them. Holiness was the means by which they enjoyed his presence and displayed his glory. The holiness code is less about rule-keeping and more about relationship.

Today, holiness still means reflecting God's character—justice, purity, mercy, and faithfulness—in a world that often despises those very virtues. True holiness never isolates; it illuminates. The Christian's life becomes a living holiness code, a testimony that the God who once dwelled in a tent now dwells in human hearts.

APPLICATION

1. Holiness shapes every relationship

The holiness code begins with worship and ends with community because holiness cannot exist in isolation. Loving God and loving people are two sides of the same coin. Israel learned that the same hands lifted in sacrifice must also feed the hungry, honor parents, and deal honestly in business. Christians too must guard against fragmented faith—praising God on Sunday but ignoring his image-bearers on Monday. True holiness changes how we speak, treat others, and handle power. It reaches from the sanctuary to the supper table. When believers practice fairness, forgiveness, and faithfulness, they proclaim that God still dwells among his people. Holiness is not withdrawal from others but the presence of God made visible through kindness, integrity, and truth.

2. The sacredness of life and the power of the blood

Leviticus 17 taught Israel that blood belongs to God because life belongs to God. Every heartbeat was a divine gift. By respecting blood, the Israelites learned to respect the sanctity of all life—human and animal. Christians must recover that same reverence. In a world that cheapens life through violence, exploitation, or indifference, holiness values every person as one made in God's image. But the lesson goes deeper: blood atones. The blood of Christ does not simply cover sin—it conquers it. Every communion cup reminds believers that holiness and mercy flow together at the cross. The sacredness of life finds its fullest meaning in the life that was freely given for ours.

3. Moral purity reflects God's character

The commands of Leviticus 18 may seem ancient, but they rest on eternal truth: holiness guards intimacy. Sexual sin distorts what God designed for covenant faithfulness and love. In every generation, believers must resist a culture that celebrates indulgence and calls it freedom. Holiness protects rather than deprives. When Christians pursue purity, they mirror the faithfulness of the God who keeps his promises. This obedience is not fear-driven but love-driven; we choose restraint because we cherish relationships. The Spirit empowers believers to live counterculturally—to honor marriage, flee temptation, and find joy in obedience. Holiness in the body and heart declares to the world that belonging to God changes everything about how we love.

4. Be holy because you belong

The refrain "You shall be holy, for I am holy" appears again and again because identity drives behavior. Israel was holy because God chose them; they lived differently because they were his. The same truth defines Christians today. We do not pursue holiness to earn acceptance but because we already have it in Christ. Grace does not lower the standard—it enables us to meet it. The more we understand who we are—redeemed, cleansed, and called—the more naturally we will reflect the One who saved us. Holiness is family resemblance. God's children should look like their Father. Every act of kindness, purity, and justice says to the world, "We belong to him."

CONCLUSION

Leviticus 17–20 shows that holiness is not an event but a way of life. The God who dwelled in the tabernacle wanted his people's hearts, homes, and habits to reflect his purity. Worship, morality, and justice were never separate categories—they were all part of life with God.

For Christians, the holiness code is not a relic but a mirror. It reveals what happens when grace shapes conduct and belonging fuels obedience. Through the Spirit, believers embody the same refrain that echoed through Israel's camp: "Be holy, for I am holy."

Next, Leviticus 21–22 will narrow the focus from the nation to its priests, showing that those who serve must model the holiness of God.

REFLECTION

1. Why was blood considered sacred in Israel's worship?
2. What moral boundaries did God give to protect family and community?
3. How does Leviticus 19 connect holiness with justice and compassion?
4. Why did God demand separation from Canaanite practices?
5. How does Peter apply Leviticus' command to "be holy"?
6. What do these chapters teach about holiness as a relationship, not a ritual?

DISCUSSION

1. How can holiness shape your relationships with others?
2. What does the sacredness of life mean in today's world?
3. How can Christians pursue purity in a culture that mocks restraint?
4. What modern practices threaten the church's moral integrity?
5. How does belonging to God motivate obedience rather than fear?
6. How can your home and work reflect the character of a holy God?

8

SACRED SERVICE
LEVITICUS 21–22

Objective: To recognize that serving a holy God requires integrity, reverence, and wholehearted devotion.

INTRODUCTION

In 1924, a Scottish sprinter named Eric Liddell qualified for the Olympic 100-meter race. But when he learned the final would be held on a Sunday, he refused to run. Many called him foolish; others accused him of betraying his country. Yet Liddell believed that honoring God was worth more than winning gold. He later competed in another event and, to everyone's surprise, won. But more than medals, it was his conviction that made history—service to God demands sacred integrity.

Leviticus 21–22 speaks that same truth. The priests of Israel were set apart to represent God's holiness before the people. Their behavior, marriages, and even their meals were governed by his standards. To serve a holy God required holy lives. These chapters remind us that closeness to God carries both privilege and responsibility.

In Christ, every believer now shares that priestly calling. We are not bound by Levitical rules, yet we still serve before the same God whose name must never be profaned. Sacred service means reflecting his holiness in how we lead, love, and live.

EXAMINATION

Holiness in representation (21:1-2)

Leviticus 21-22 turns the focus from the holiness of the people to the holiness of their priests. These men stood between God and Israel, offering sacrifices and prayers on behalf of the nation. Their lives, therefore, had to embody the very character of the God they represented. As the Lord said, "Speak to the priests, the sons of Aaron, and say to them: No one shall make himself unclean for the dead among his people" (21:1).

Holiness for the priests was not optional. They were living symbols of divine purity and mercy. The closer one stood to God's presence, the greater the demand for reverence. Leviticus 21-22 outlines those expectations in two areas: personal conduct and sacrificial practice. Through these laws, Israel learned that worship is not only what happens at the altar—it's also how the worshiper lives beyond it.

The priest's conduct (21:1-15)

The first section governs the priest's relationship to death, marriage, and family. Ordinary Israelites could mourn freely for loved ones, but priests had to show restraint. They could become ceremonially unclean only for immediate relatives—father, mother, son, daughter, brother, or unmarried sister (21:1-3). To touch a corpse or join in pagan mourning rituals would profane their sacred office. Their grief, though real, had to remain distinct from the customs of the nations around them.

The restriction reflected a profound truth: priests represented life before a God who is the source of life. Contact with death symbolized separation from that life. The same principle applied to their appearance: no shaving of heads, trimming of beards, or cutting of flesh (21:5)—practices linked with idolatrous mourning. Their holiness was to be visible, not theatrical.

Marriage regulations also reinforced purity. Priests could marry only virgins or widows of priests (21:7, 13-15). The priest's home mirrored his calling; his family life had to reflect the same sanctity as his service. The high priest, in particular, bore stricter standards. He could not mourn publicly even for his parents nor leave the sanctuary during duty (21:10-12). His consecration was unique: "The anointing oil of his God is on him."

These commands were not about privilege but responsibility. The high priest carried the nation's sins into the presence of God; his life had to embody the holiness of that ministry.

Physical wholeness and service (21:16–24)

The next section addresses physical defects that disqualified priests from offering sacrifices. "No man who has a blemish shall draw near" (21:18). The list includes blindness, lameness, deformity, and other visible impairments. However, these men were not cast out or shamed. They could still eat the holy food and live within the sanctuary community (21:22). The restriction applied only to public service at the altar.

This rule symbolized God's perfection. The physical integrity of the priest reflected the moral integrity of the God he served. Every act of worship pointed to wholeness—no flaw in the offering, no defect in the mediator, no blemish in the sacrifice. Yet this regulation also revealed the longing for a priest without defect, one perfectly fit to represent humanity before God.

That longing finds its answer in Christ, "a high priest, holy, innocent, unstained, separated from sinners" (Heb. 7:26). The physical wholeness required in Leviticus pointed to the moral and spiritual perfection fulfilled in him.

The sacredness of the offerings (22:1–16)

Chapter 22 expands the theme of holiness to the offerings themselves. The priests had to treat sacred food—the portions of sacrifices reserved for them—with reverence. If a priest was ceremonially unclean, he could not eat of the holy things until he was purified (22:4–7). To do otherwise would "profane my holy name" (22:2).

This insistence on purity protected both the dignity of God and the blessing of his people. The priest's carelessness could bring guilt upon the nation. The Lord's holiness required attention to detail: "They shall therefore keep my charge, lest they bear sin for it and die thereby when they profane it" (22:9).

The law also safeguarded access. Only priests and members of their households could eat from the holy food; hired workers and guests could not (22:10–13). Yet provision was made for widows or daughters who returned home—they could again share in the sacred portions. Holiness was firm but compassionate.

These instructions emphasized that holiness is not inherited automatically; it must be honored through obedience. Sacred things remain sacred only when treated as such.

Unblemished sacrifices (22:17–33)

If priests had to be without defect, so too did the animals they offered. "Whatever has a blemish, you shall not offer, for it will not be acceptable for you" (22:20). Only animals that were whole and sound could represent the holiness of the Lord. Blind, injured, or mutilated animals dishonored God. Worship demanded the best.

The principle extended beyond ritual: God deserves excellence, not leftovers. To offer less was to insult his worth. The prophet Malachi would later rebuke the priests of his day for bringing lame and sick animals, asking, "Present that to your governor; will he accept you or show you favor?" (Mal. 1:8).

Leviticus also commands gratitude. Offerings given in fulfillment of vows or as freewill gifts had to meet the same standard (22:21–23). Worship was never to be cheap or careless. Holiness demanded intention.

The chapter concludes with a theological summary: "You shall not profane my holy name, that I may be sanctified among the people of Israel. I am the Lord who sanctifies you, who brought you out of the land of Egypt to be your God" (22:32–33). Holiness, then, is not human achievement but a divine gift. God sanctifies his people, calling them to reflect his character through reverent obedience.

Holiness, representation, and perfection

The priesthood embodied three great truths about holiness. First, holiness is relational. The priests' restrictions were not arbitrary; they were relational boundaries that safeguarded communion with God. Every command about mourning, marriage, or food preserved the integrity of worship so that God's presence could dwell among his people.

Second, holiness is representative. The priest did not act for himself but for the nation. His purity or impurity affected everyone. This principle echoes through Scripture: leaders carry the weight of representation. Those who teach, shepherd, or serve bear a visible testimony to God's character. Holiness in leadership is not perfectionism—it is faithfulness to reflect the One we serve.

Third, holiness is perfected in Christ. Every priestly regulation pointed beyond human frailty to divine completion. The high priest's careful preparation foreshadowed the perfect obedience of Jesus. The unblemished animals anticipated the Lamb "without blemish or spot" (1 Pet. 1:19). The call to avoid defilement anticipated the sinlessness of the One who "knew no sin" yet became sin for us (2 Cor. 5:21).

Through Christ, the holiness once restricted to the priests now extends to all believers. We are "a royal priesthood" (1 Pet. 2:9), consecrated not by lineage but by grace.

Modern application of priestly holiness

While Christians no longer follow the ceremonial regulations of Leviticus, the principles behind them remain vital. Those who serve God—whether in public ministry or daily discipleship—are called to reflect his holiness in conduct, compassion, and character.

Holiness in Conduct. The priest's discipline around death and mourning teaches believers to distinguish between grief that honors God and despair that forgets him. We grieve with hope (1 Thess. 4:13). Our emotions, like our actions, belong under his lordship.

Holiness in Relationships. The priest's home was an extension of his service. Likewise, Christian leaders and disciples alike must model faithfulness, humility, and purity. Family life and ministry integrity are not separate—they are intertwined.

Holiness in Worship. The priest's care for the holy things warns believers against casual worship. The church gathers before the same holy God. Reverence, joy, and gratitude should mark our approach.

Holiness still begins at the altar—but now that altar is the heart cleansed by Christ's blood.

Fulfillment in Christ and the church's priesthood

The Levitical priesthood finds its culmination in Jesus Christ. Hebrews 7–10 explains that the old order was temporary, "for the law appoints men in their weakness as high priests, but the word of the oath appoints a Son who has been made perfect forever" (Heb. 7:28).

Jesus fulfills every qualification: sinless in life, flawless in offering, perfect in obedience. His death achieved what generations of priests could not—eternal redemption. Unlike the sons of Aaron, he never needed to offer sacrifices for his own sins. He entered heaven itself as both priest and sacrifice, once for all.

Through him, the church inherits a new kind of priesthood. Every believer serves as a priest, offering spiritual sacrifices of praise, service, and compassion. "You yourselves like living stones are being built up as a spiritual house, to be a holy priesthood" (1 Pet. 2:5).

The church's leaders—elders, preachers, teachers—bear special responsibility to model holiness, but all Christians share the same calling. The standards of Leviticus 21–22 still speak: God's representatives must honor his name through integrity and reverence.

Holiness, however, is no longer enforced through ritual separation but expressed through Christlike love. The perfect priest now dwells within his people, transforming their hearts into sanctuaries of his presence.

The beauty of holiness

Leviticus 21–22 teaches that holiness is not a burden but a blessing. God's commands protected his priests from corruption and preserved his people's access to grace. In the same way, holiness today protects believers from spiritual decay. To live reverently before God is to live freely under his favor.

When the church reflects the beauty of holiness—through purity, humility, and sincerity—it becomes a living testimony to the God who still sanctifies. The priestly call of Leviticus continues not in robes and rituals but in hearts and hands devoted to sacred service.

APPLICATION

1. Holiness requires integrity in every role

The priests were not allowed to divide their lives into "sacred" and "ordinary." Every decision, from how they mourned to whom they married, reflected the character of the God they served. Christians face the same calling. Our work, relationships, and habits either magnify or diminish the holiness of God before others. Whether leading a congregation, teaching children, or running a business, integrity is sacred service. We live before a watching world that learns about God's holiness through our example. As

Paul wrote, "Whatever you do, do all to the glory of God" (1 Cor. 10:31). The standard of Leviticus remains: those who represent God must mirror his character. Holiness is not perfection—it is consistent devotion that guards his name with reverence.

2. God deserves our best, not our leftovers

Unblemished animals were the only acceptable offerings because they symbolized God's perfection and worth. The principle endures: the Lord deserves excellence, not convenience. Worship that costs nothing dishonors the One who gave everything. Christians must resist the temptation to give God what is easy—rushed prayers, distracted hearts, or minimal service. Holiness means offering our best time, energy, and resources as acts of gratitude. When we bring excellence to worship, work, and service, we proclaim that God is worth every effort. Romans 12:1 calls us to present our bodies "as a living sacrifice, holy and acceptable to God." The altar may no longer burn with fire, but the same standard applies. Holiness gives God our first and finest, not what's left over.

3. Those who serve must reflect the One they serve

The priest's life was not his own. He stood before God for the people and before the people for God. That dual calling demanded humility, purity, and example. The same is true for all who serve in Christ's name. Leaders, teachers, parents, and ministers represent God's character to others. Holiness in service isn't about rank but reflection—allowing others to glimpse the heart of Christ through our words and actions. When our conduct contradicts our confession, we profane the name we bear. The church's witness depends on the credibility of its servants. That's why Paul urged Timothy, "Keep yourself pure" (1 Tim. 5:22). Sacred service begins not in public tasks but in private character. A clean heart is the truest uniform of the priesthood.

4. Christ makes us whole to serve

Leviticus excluded priests with physical defects from the altar, symbolizing that service required wholeness. In Christ, the symbol becomes reality. He restores what sin has damaged, making us fit for ministry. Our weaknesses no longer disqualify us; they become instruments of grace. The gospel transforms blemished people into holy servants. Through forgiveness, broken lives are made whole, and flawed voices proclaim his glory. God doesn't demand physical perfection but spiritual devotion. The church is a living picture of this truth—ordinary believers cleansed and commissioned for sacred work. Paul reminds us that "we have this treasure in jars of clay" (2 Cor. 4:7). The perfection of our service lies not in us, but in the perfect High Priest who sanctifies us for his purposes.

CONCLUSION

Leviticus 21–22 reminds us that sacred service flows from sacred character. The priests were not holy because they wore special garments, but because they represented a holy God. Every command about mourning, marriage, or sacrifice protected the integrity of worship and the honor of God's name.

In Christ, holiness is no longer confined to the priesthood—it belongs to every believer. We serve not through ritual but through lives purified by grace. The God who once said, "You shall not profane my holy name," now calls his people to glorify it through humility, excellence, and love.

Next, Leviticus 23 will shift from priestly conduct to holy time, revealing how Israel's feasts celebrated redemption, rest, and the rhythm of God's grace.

REFLECTION

1. Why were priests held to higher standards than the rest of Israel?
2. What did contact with death symbolize for those serving God?
3. Why did priests and sacrifices both have to be without blemish?
4. How did the priest's purity affect the whole community's worship?
5. What does it mean that God "sanctifies" his people?
6. How does Christ fulfill the role of the perfect, unblemished priest?

DISCUSSION

1. What does integrity look like in your role as a servant of God?
2. How can we give God our best rather than our leftovers?
3. What habits help believers keep their worship reverent and focused?
4. How can Christian leaders reflect God's holiness in humility and grace?
5. How does Christ's healing of our brokenness equip us for ministry?
6. What practical steps can the church take to model sacred service today?

9

HOLY TIME
LEVITICUS 23

Objective: To understand how Israel's feasts reveal God's rhythm of rest, gratitude, and redemption fulfilled in Christ.

INTRODUCTION

In the small town of Assisi, Italy, a centuries-old clock still chimes every hour—but not for tourists. It rings for monks who pause whatever they're doing to pray. Their rhythm of life isn't driven by deadlines but by devotion. Time itself has become an act of worship.

Leviticus 23 presents a similar picture. God taught Israel that time belongs to him. The feasts were more than dates on a calendar—they were reminders that every season of life flows from God's grace. Work, rest, planting, and harvest were all woven into the story of redemption. Through these sacred days, God gave his people a rhythm of remembrance: to rest in his provision, to rejoice in his salvation, and to renew their covenant with him.

For Christians, these ancient festivals still speak. Every Lord's Day, every communion table, and every act of thanksgiving continues the same song of redemption. God is not just the Lord of space—he is the Lord of time. Holiness begins when we let him order our days.

EXAMINATION

Time made holy (23:1-2)

Leviticus 23 moves from holy places and holy people to holy time. God commanded Israel not only to worship in certain ways, but also to remember him at certain times. "The Lord spoke to Moses, saying, 'Speak to the people of Israel and say to them, These are the appointed feasts of the Lord that you shall proclaim as holy convocations; they are my appointed feasts'" (23:1-2).

Time itself was to be consecrated. These "appointed times" shaped Israel's calendar, creating a rhythm of work, rest, and remembrance. Every week, month, and year reminded them that life was a gift sustained by the God who had redeemed them from Egypt. The feasts were not mere holidays; they were rehearsals of God's story. Each one recalled a moment of salvation history and invited the people to participate in it anew.

Sabbath: The rhythm of rest (23:3)

Before describing the annual festivals, God began with the weekly Sabbath: "Six days shall work be done, but on the seventh day is a Sabbath of solemn rest, a holy convocation" (23:3). The Sabbath anchored all the feasts—it was a weekly reminder that holiness begins with rest in God's provision.

Israel's neighbors worshiped through endless labor to appease their gods, but Yahweh invited his people to rest in his completed work. Sabbath was not laziness; it was trust. It declared that life does not depend on human striving but divine faithfulness.

In Christ, that rhythm finds fulfillment. The writer of Hebrews speaks of a greater rest: "So then, there remains a Sabbath rest for the people of God" (Heb. 4:9). Every Lord's Day, Christians gather to remember that our salvation is not earned but received. The Sabbath principle still whispers to restless souls: stop, remember, and rejoice in the God who provides.

Passover: Redemption remembered (23:4-8)

The first annual feast, Passover, occurred on the fourteenth day of the first month. It commemorated the night God delivered Israel from Egypt when the blood of the lamb shielded their homes from judgment (Exod. 12).

Immediately following Passover came the Feast of Unleavened Bread, lasting seven days. During that week, no leaven could be eaten or even kept in the house.

Together, these feasts celebrated redemption and renewal—deliverance from bondage and the call to purity. Leaven symbolized corruption and haste; removing it reminded Israel that salvation demands separation from sin.

In the New Testament, Paul explicitly connects this feast to Christ: "Christ, our Passover lamb, has been sacrificed. Therefore let us keep the feast… with the unleavened bread of sincerity and truth" (1 Cor. 5:7–8). At the cross, the blood of the Lamb once again turned away judgment. In the Lord's Supper, believers continue to remember that redemption has a price and purity has a purpose.

Firstfruits: Provision and gratitude (23:9–14)

The Feast of Firstfruits followed soon after Passover. When the Israelites entered the Promised Land, they were to bring the first sheaf of their harvest to the priest, who would wave it before the Lord as an offering of thanksgiving (23:10–11). No bread or roasted grain could be eaten until this act of gratitude was complete.

The principle was clear: the first belongs to God. The firstfruits acknowledged that the whole harvest came from him. It was a pledge of trust and thanksgiving before the rest of the fields were even reaped.

This feast foreshadowed the resurrection of Christ. Paul writes, "But in fact Christ has been raised from the dead, the firstfruits of those who have fallen asleep" (1 Cor. 15:20). Just as the first sheaf guaranteed a greater harvest to come, Jesus' resurrection guarantees ours. Each Sunday—the day of resurrection—becomes a weekly Firstfruits celebration, when Christians offer themselves to God in gratitude for new life.

Pentecost: The joy of harvest (23:15–22)

Fifty days after Firstfruits came the Feast of Weeks, also known as Pentecost. It marked the end of the grain harvest and celebrated God's abundant provision. The people brought two loaves of bread made with leaven, offered alongside sacrifices and a communal meal (23:17–20).

Unlike the unleavened bread of Passover, these loaves contained yeast—symbolizing completion and fellowship. The feast joined gratitude with generosity: "When you reap the harvest of your land, you shall not reap your field right up to its edge… you shall leave them for the poor and for the sojourner" (23:22). God's blessing always carried a call to compassion.

In Acts 2, the Feast of Weeks reached its true fulfillment. On the day of Pentecost, the Spirit descended on the apostles, and the first fruits of the church were gathered. What began as an agricultural festival became the celebration of spiritual harvest. The law given at Sinai found its counterpart in the Spirit given in Jerusalem. The covenant written on stone became the covenant written on hearts.

Trumpets: The call to renewal (23:23–25)

The Feast of Trumpets (later called Rosh Hashanah) began the seventh month, a time of reflection and renewal. "You shall observe a day of solemn rest, a memorial proclaimed with blast of trumpets, a holy convocation" (23:24). The trumpet blasts called the nation to awaken—to prepare for the coming Day of Atonement.

The feast marked both a civil new year and a spiritual reset. The trumpet's sound was a summons to remember God's faithfulness and repent of neglect. It was both celebration and warning: joy that God reigns and reminder that judgment draws near.

In the New Testament, trumpets often signal God's final intervention. Paul writes, "The trumpet will sound, and the dead will be raised imperishable" (1 Cor. 15:52). For Christians, every trumpet in Scripture echoes the same message: wake up, remember, and be ready.

Yom Kippur: The cleansing of the nation (23:26–32)

Ten days after the Feast of Trumpets came the Day of Atonement (Yom Kippur), described earlier in detail in Leviticus 16. It was the most solemn day of the year—a day of fasting, humility, and forgiveness. "You shall afflict yourselves and do no work… for on this day shall atonement be made for you to cleanse you" (23:27–28).

The feast calendar placed Atonement between the trumpet's warning and the tabernacle's joy, reminding Israel that cleansing always precedes celebration. No one could approach the Feast of Booths without first being purified. The day renewed Israel's fellowship with God and reaffirmed the seriousness of sin.

For Christians, the Day of Atonement finds its fulfillment in the cross. Christ entered not the earthly tabernacle but the heavenly one, "having obtained eternal redemption" (Heb. 9:12). His blood made the final atonement so that our lives can become perpetual days of grace and gratitude.

Booths: The joy of dwelling (23:33–44)

The final feast, Booths (or Tabernacles), completed the year's cycle. For seven days, Israel dwelled in temporary shelters made of branches, recalling their wilderness journey after leaving Egypt. "You shall dwell in booths… that your generations may know that I made the people of Israel dwell in booths when I brought them out of the land of Egypt" (23:42–43).

Booths was the most joyful of all feasts. It marked the harvest's completion and the memory of God's provision in the desert. Families rejoiced together under the open sky, giving thanks for the God who turned tents into homes and wanderers into a nation.

This feast pointed toward the ultimate dwelling of God with his people. John declares, "The Word became flesh and dwelt among us" (John 1:14)—literally, "tabernacled" among us. And Revelation 21 completes the picture: "Behold, the dwelling place of God is with man." What began in tents ends in eternal communion. Booths was the festival of joy; its fulfillment is heaven itself.

The pattern of holy time

The seven feasts together tell Israel's story—from redemption to rest, from harvest to holiness, from wilderness to worship. They form a sacred rhythm:

- Passover and Unleavened Bread: Redemption from bondage.
- Firstfruits: Resurrection and hope.
- Weeks (Pentecost): Provision and covenant renewal.
- Trumpets: Awakening and repentance.
- Atonement: Cleansing and reconciliation.
- Booths: Joy and God's dwelling.

Each step mirrors the gospel. God redeems, provides, calls, forgives, and dwells with his people. Time itself becomes a testimony of grace. The feasts were not an escape from life but a sanctification of it. They taught Israel to see God in every season.

Christians still need that rhythm. In an age that prizes busyness and forgets rest, we need sacred pauses—moments that remind us who we are and whose we are. Weekly worship and the Lord's Supper carry the same function: to remember redemption and renew joy.

Fulfillment in Christ: The Lord of time

Every feast in Leviticus 23 points to Christ. He is the Passover Lamb, the Unleavened Bread of sincerity, the Firstfruits of resurrection, the Giver of the Spirit at Pentecost, the Trumpet who awakens the dead, the Atonement who cleanses sin, and the Tabernacle where God dwells with his people.

Jesus sanctifies not only space but time. His death, resurrection, and return reshape history itself. For the Christian, every day becomes holy because every moment can be lived in his presence. The feasts that once punctuated Israel's year now pulse within the believer's life.

The rhythm of Leviticus 23 ends with joy—God dwelling with his people. That same joy fuels Christian hope. The one who turned the cross into a feast of forgiveness will one day turn all time into eternity.

APPLICATION

1. Remember God's rhythm of rest

The Sabbath and the feasts reminded Israel that time belongs to God. In a world that measures worth by productivity, God commands rest. Sabbath wasn't a break from holiness but a celebration of it—it declared that life depends on grace, not grind. Christians honor this rhythm by keeping sacred pauses in their week. The Lord's Day is not a leftover of the past but a living testimony that Christ has finished his work. Setting apart time for worship, prayer, and fellowship trains our hearts to trust instead of hurry. Rest is not laziness; it is faith expressed in time. To rest in God is to remember that the world spins because he sustains it, not because we do.

2. Celebrate redemption with gratitude and purity

Passover and Unleavened Bread taught Israel to remember salvation and remove corruption. Every year they relived the night when God redeemed them from slavery. Christians celebrate that same deliverance through Christ, our Passover Lamb. Each time we partake of the Lord's Supper, we proclaim that his blood protects us and his body sustains us. But redemption calls for response. Just as leaven was removed from Israelite homes, sin must be removed from Christian hearts. Gratitude without repentance becomes hypocrisy. The feast teaches that holiness and joy belong together: we rejoice in salvation while cleansing our lives of the old yeast of sin. A redeemed people must live like they've been freed.

3. Live generously as a harvest people

The Feasts of Firstfruits and Weeks celebrated God's provision. The Israelites gave their first and best to acknowledge that all they owned came from his hand. Their harvest generosity extended to the poor, who could glean from the edges of their fields. The same principle governs Christian stewardship. Everything we have—time, money, talent, and opportunity—is harvest from God's grace. We honor him by offering the first, not the leftovers. Generosity isn't a budget issue; it's a holiness issue. When we give joyfully, we declare that God is our provider. Pentecost shows that harvests aren't just grain—they're souls. Every act of giving fuels the mission of gathering the world into God's kingdom. Holiness shares what it's received.

4. Rejoice in the God who dwells with us

The Feast of Booths celebrated God's presence during Israel's wilderness journey. Families lived in tents for a week, remembering that even in temporary shelters, God was near. For Christians, this feast reminds us that joy isn't tied to comfort but to communion. We live as pilgrims, yet never alone—the Word became flesh and "tabernacled" among us. Through the Spirit, God dwells not in tents but in hearts. Our gatherings, meals, and worship echo the Feast of Booths every time we celebrate his faithfulness together. Joyful holiness means remembering that our true home is coming. Until then, every table can become an altar, every day a feast, and every believer a living reminder that God still walks with his people.

CONCLUSION

Leviticus 23 reveals that holiness isn't just about sacred places or people—

it's about sacred time. God taught Israel to mark every season with gratitude, rest, and renewal. Each feast told part of their story: redemption at Passover, provision at Pentecost, and joy in God's presence at Booths. Together, they formed a calendar of grace.

For Christians, these feasts point to Christ—the Lamb, the Firstfruits, the Giver of the Spirit, and the eternal Tabernacle of God's presence. Our lives now follow his rhythm: resting in his finished work, rejoicing in his grace, and waiting for his return.

Next, Leviticus 24 will focus on light, bread, and justice—symbols of God's continual presence among his people.

REFLECTION

1. Why did God command Israel to mark time with feasts and rest days?
2. How did the Sabbath shape Israel's trust in God's provision?
3. What truths did Passover and Unleavened Bread teach about redemption?
4. How did Firstfruits and Weeks express gratitude and dependence?
5. What role did the Feast of Booths play in Israel's worship?
6. How does Christ fulfill the meaning of all Israel's feasts?

DISCUSSION

1. How can Christians rediscover the rhythm of rest and worship today?
2. What are some practical ways to remember redemption daily?
3. How can generosity become an act of holiness in modern life?
4. What habits help us celebrate God's presence in ordinary time?
5. How do our church gatherings echo Israel's feasts of joy and renewal?
6. In what ways can you turn your home into a place of worship?

10

LIGHT, BREAD, & BLASPHEMY
LEVITICUS 24

Objective: To understand how God's continual presence calls Christians to worship, reverence, and justice.

INTRODUCTION

When the great cathedrals of Europe were built, craftsmen designed massive stained-glass windows that only revealed their beauty when sunlight streamed through them. In the dark, the glass seemed dull and ordinary. But when illuminated, every color came alive. Light made the difference—it transformed stone and glass into a vision of glory.

Leviticus 24 is about that kind of light—the radiance of God's holiness shining through ordinary elements. Inside the tabernacle, the golden lamp burned continually, and the bread of the Presence was always set before the Lord. These symbols proclaimed that God's presence was constant, his provision unending, and his name worthy of reverence. Even when the camp slept, the light still burned.

Yet holiness wasn't confined to the sanctuary. When an Israelite blasphemed God's name, he defiled that same holiness. The chapter ends with laws of justice, reminding Israel that worship and daily life are inseparable. The God whose light fills the tabernacle must also guide the heart.

EXAMINATION

The sanctuary of everyday holiness (24:1–2)

Leviticus 24 stands as a pause between the annual rhythms of Israel's worship (ch. 23) and the sabbatical and jubilee years that follow (ch. 25). Having described the holy times, God now turns to the holy space—the tabernacle, where his presence was continually remembered through light and bread. The chapter moves from devotion (vv. 1–9) to discipline (vv. 10–23), reminding Israel that the same God who provides light for worship also demands reverence in speech and conduct.

"The Lord spoke to Moses, saying, 'Command the people of Israel to bring you pure oil from beaten olives for the lamp, that a light may be kept burning regularly'" (24:1–2). Holiness required not only sacred days but daily faithfulness. The priests were to tend the lamp and arrange the bread "regularly before the Lord." In these ongoing acts, Israel learned that holiness was not occasional but constant—a light that never went out, a table that was never empty, and a name that was never profaned.

The lamp of God's presence (24:1–4)

The first section focuses on the golden lampstand (*menorah*) inside the tabernacle. Aaron and his sons were to keep its seven lamps burning continually, using "pure oil from beaten olives." The light illuminated the Holy Place, symbolizing God's continual presence and guidance among his people.

In the ancient world, perpetual lamps burned in royal palaces and temples as signs of life and protection. In Israel, the light had deeper meaning: it represented the presence of the living God who neither slumbers nor sleeps. The lamp burned "from evening to morning before the Lord," showing that even through the night, God watched over his people.

The lamp also reminded Israel of their calling. They were to be a nation of light in a dark world (Isa. 42:6). The priest tended the flame, but the people supplied the oil. Holiness, therefore, was both communal and continual. It was sustained by obedience and fueled by devotion.

In the New Testament, the symbolism is fulfilled in Christ: "I am the light of the world" (John 8:12). The tabernacle lamp foreshadowed his radiance, the glory that no darkness can overcome. Through him, believers become lamps themselves—"the light of the world" (Matt. 5:14). Just as

Aaron trimmed the wicks and replenished the oil, so Christians must keep their faith burning through prayer, Scripture, and obedience. The holy lamp teaches that the light of God is not meant to flicker but to shine continually.

The bread of the covenant (24:5–9)

Beside the lampstand stood another enduring symbol: the table of the bread of the Presence. Each Sabbath, twelve loaves of fine flour were baked and arranged in two rows of six "before the Lord." They were set on a pure table with frankincense as a memorial portion. At the end of the week, the priests ate the old loaves in a holy place, and new bread replaced them.

This bread—literally "the bread of the face"—represented fellowship with God. Just as a shared meal signified friendship, so the continual offering of bread reminded Israel that the Lord dwelled among them and sustained them. The number twelve symbolized the twelve tribes, all represented equally before him.

The bread's weekly renewal symbolized both God's provision and Israel's gratitude. Every Sabbath, the covenant relationship was reaffirmed—God feeding his people, his people honoring God. It also taught that holiness must be nourished regularly. Just as physical bread sustains the body, spiritual communion sustains the soul.

In the Gospel of John, Jesus again fulfills this image: "I am the bread of life" (John 6:35). The loaves on the table pointed forward to him—the true sustenance of God's people. Through him, fellowship with God becomes continual. The church's weekly communion echoes this rhythm of renewal, reminding believers that God's presence is not a memory but a meal we still share.

The blasphemer's sin (24:10–16)

From the sanctuary's calm we suddenly move to a courtroom crisis. The story of the blasphemer seems abrupt, but it illustrates what happens when holiness is profaned. "Now an Israelite woman's son, whose father was an Egyptian, went out among the people of Israel. And the Israelite woman's son and a man of Israel fought in the camp, and the son of the Israelite woman blasphemed the Name, and cursed" (24:10–11).

The offender, born of a mixed household, symbolizes divided allegiance. In anger, he "blasphemed the Name"—not just any name, but the sacred covenant Name of Yahweh, which Jews later refused even to pronounce. He was seized and placed in custody until the Lord's will was made clear. The verdict came through Moses: "Whoever blasphemes the name of the Lord shall surely be put to death" (24:16).

Why such severity? Because to curse God's name was to attack the very foundation of holiness. The lamp and bread represented the Lord's presence and provision; blasphemy denied both. To despise the Name was to reject the covenant. In Israel, words were not trivial—they carried the power of life and death.

This episode taught that God's presence is not to be taken lightly. The holiness of the tabernacle extended into daily speech. The people who heard the priest bless in God's name (Num. 6:24–26) were also responsible to honor that name in their own.

For Christians, the principle remains: reverence for God begins with our words. Jesus taught that careless speech flows from careless hearts (Matt. 12:36–37). To profane God's name is to contradict the gospel we proclaim. When we pray, "Hallowed be your name," we commit ourselves to living and speaking in ways that magnify rather than mock his holiness.

The justice of God (24:17–23)

After the blasphemy case, God reaffirmed the principles of justice that sustain holiness in society. These laws, echoing earlier commands (Exod. 21), establish fairness and restraint. "Whoever takes a human life shall surely be put to death… fracture for fracture, eye for eye, tooth for tooth" (24:17–20).

The phrase "eye for eye" has often been misunderstood as a call for vengeance. In reality, it was the opposite—a safeguard against excessive retaliation. It ensured proportional justice, limiting punishment to the severity of the offense. Holiness required equity, not cruelty.

The laws conclude with a universal principle: "You shall have the same rule for the sojourner and for the native, for I am the Lord your God" (24:22). Justice in Israel was not to be partial. Even foreigners living among them were protected by the same law. God's holiness demanded fairness because he himself is impartial.

By ending with justice, Leviticus 24 links worship and ethics. Light and bread symbolize holiness within the sanctuary; truth and fairness embody holiness in the community. To keep the lamp burning while practicing injustice outside would make the light meaningless. Holiness at the altar must produce righteousness in the camp.

Holiness, presence, and reverence

Leviticus 24 unites three great themes of holiness: presence, provision, and reverence. The lamp and bread revealed God's nearness; the laws about blasphemy and justice protected that holiness from contempt.

Presence. The continual flame and fresh bread proclaimed that God is not distant. He dwells among his people, illuminating and feeding them. Holiness is relational before it is moral—it means living in awareness of God's constant presence.

Provision. Both symbols involved human participation. The people brought oil and flour; the priests tended and arranged. Holiness is sustained through cooperation between divine grace and human faithfulness.

Reverence. The blasphemer's punishment underscores that holiness cannot coexist with mockery. To honor God's name is to protect the dignity of worship and the integrity of community life. Reverence begins where self-centeredness ends.

When these elements—presence, provision, reverence—converge, the result is a community that reflects God's glory both in sanctuary and in society.

Fulfillment in Christ: The light, the bread, and the name

Each symbol in Leviticus 24 finds its fulfillment in Jesus Christ.

The Lamp. Jesus declared, "I am the light of the world. Whoever follows me will not walk in darkness, but will have the light of life" (John 8:12). The perpetual lamp foreshadowed his presence—constant, pure, and illuminating. At Pentecost, that light spread to the church, as tongues of fire rested on the apostles (Acts 2:3). The flame of divine presence now burns within Christians through the Spirit.

The Bread. Jesus also said, "I am the bread of life" (John 6:35). The bread of the Presence, renewed weekly, pointed to the unending fellowship believers now share in him. In the Lord's Supper, we participate in that covenant meal, remembering that our sustenance is spiritual as well as physical.

The Name. In Christ, the holiness of God's name is both revealed and restored. Through his obedience, the divine name is glorified (John 17:6).

Through his grace, sinners who once profaned that name are forgiven and invited to bear it honorably. The church now bears the name of Christ, called to speak it with awe and live it with integrity.

Together, these fulfillments show that Leviticus 24 was not about ritual maintenance but relational faithfulness. The light and bread anticipated communion; the laws on blasphemy anticipated the holiness of speech required of disciples.

Living in the light of holiness

Leviticus 24 reminds believers that holiness is continual, not seasonal. God's presence must be remembered daily, not only on feast days or in assemblies. Just as the priests tended the lamp and replaced the bread, Christians must nurture faith through prayer, worship, and service.

The chapter also warns against complacency. The blasphemer's story shows that proximity to holiness does not guarantee reverence. Familiarity can breed carelessness. Those who dwell near God's presence must guard their words and actions carefully.

Finally, the chapter teaches that holiness overflows into justice. The same God who required pure oil also required fairness for the foreigner. The light of the sanctuary must shine in the marketplace; the bread of fellowship must lead to compassion for others. Holiness that stays indoors is incomplete.

Through Christ, believers become living lamps and living loaves—sources of light and nourishment to a dark and hungry world. The same Spirit who kept the flame burning in the tabernacle now kindles holiness within the heart.

APPLICATION

1. Keep the light burning

The continual flame in the tabernacle reminded Israel that God's presence never flickers. Today, that same light burns within Christians through the Spirit. Yet even an eternal flame needs faithful tending. Prayer, Scripture, and worship are the oil that keep faith bright. When we neglect those practices, our lamps grow dim and the world grows darker. Jesus told his disciples, "Let your light shine before others" (Matt. 5:16). Holiness is visible—it should illuminate homes, workplaces, and communities. Every day offers opportunities to reflect the light of Christ through integrity, mercy, and compassion. The priests' careful attention to the lampstand teaches us that a vibrant faith is not accidental; it is maintained. Keep the flame alive, and the presence of God will shine through you.

2. Feed on God's presence daily

The bread of the Presence symbolized ongoing fellowship with God. Each Sabbath, the priests renewed it as a reminder that God continually provides. Christians enjoy that same communion through Christ, the living bread. But fellowship grows stale when it is not renewed. Regular worship and communion are not mere rituals—they are nourishment. When we partake of the Lord's Supper or spend time in Scripture, we are fed by the same God who sustained Israel in the wilderness. The bread was always before the Lord; our hearts should always be before him too. Faith is sustained not by occasional feasts but by daily dependence. When we make time to "taste and see that the Lord is good" (Psa. 34:8), we find that holiness satisfies the soul.

3. Honor the name you bear

The story of the blasphemer warns that proximity to holiness demands reverence. Israel learned that God's name must never be treated lightly; Christians bear that same name through Christ. Every word we speak and every action we take reflects the reputation of our Lord. To use his name carelessly is to dishonor the covenant we claim. Paul urged believers to live "in a manner worthy of the calling" they received (Eph. 4:1). That means our speech should heal, not harm; bless, not curse. When others hear us speak with integrity, patience, and truth, they hear the echo of holiness. The lamp and bread showed God's presence; our words should do the same. Holiness begins in the heart but is revealed through the tongue.

4. Let holiness shape your justice

Leviticus 24 ends with laws of fairness because holiness cannot stop at the altar—it must shape daily life. God's justice was impartial: the same law for the Israelite and the foreigner. True holiness produces integrity in every relationship. Christians cannot claim to worship a holy God while tolerating dishonesty, prejudice, or cruelty. The church's light must shine brightest in the way it treats people. When believers forgive freely, speak truthfully, and act compassionately, they demonstrate that God's righteousness is not theory but practice. Micah summarized it well: "Do justice, love kindness, and walk humbly with your God" (Mic. 6:8). Holiness without justice is hypocrisy, but holiness that loves its neighbor reveals the heart of God to the world.

CONCLUSION

Leviticus 24 draws holiness down to daily life. The lamp and the bread proclaimed God's continual presence, while the laws about speech and justice protected that holiness from being profaned. Worship in Israel was not confined to sacred space—it flowed into sacred character.

For Christians, these symbols find their fulfillment in Christ, the light of the world and the bread of life. His presence burns within his people, illuminating their words, work, and witness. To live before a holy God is to let that light shine and that bread satisfy others.

Next, Leviticus 25 will reveal how holiness shapes years as well as days—through rest, release, and the jubilee of God's grace.

REFLECTION

1. What did the continual lamp symbolize about God's presence in Israel?
2. How did the bread of the Presence express fellowship between God and his people?
3. Why was blasphemy treated so seriously in Israel's law?
4. How does Leviticus 24 link worship and justice?
5. What three themes summarize holiness in this chapter?
6. How does Christ fulfill the light, bread, and name of Leviticus 24?

DISCUSSION

1. How can believers keep their spiritual "lamps" burning brightly today?
2. What practices help you feed regularly on God's presence?
3. How can Christians honor God's name in speech and conduct?
4. What does holiness look like in our treatment of others?
5. How can the church reflect both reverence and compassion in daily life?
6. Which image—light, bread, or name—best captures your current walk with God?

11

FREEDOM & REST

LEVITICUS 25

Objective: To learn how rest, release, and renewal express faith in God's ownership and provision.

INTRODUCTION

In 1949, a small farm in Kansas faced a year of drought. The ground cracked, the wells dried, and the farmer's faith wavered. Yet when his neighbors urged him to plow deeper and plant anyway, he refused. He said, "The land needs a rest—God will send rain when it's ready." Months later, the storms came, and his fields flourished. When asked why he waited, he smiled and said, "It's not my land—it's his."

Leviticus 25 captures that same spirit of faith. God commanded Israel to rest the land every seventh year and to celebrate liberty every fiftieth. These laws were not about agriculture or economics—they were about trust. A holy nation was to live by rhythms of rest, release, and renewal. The Sabbath year taught dependence; the Jubilee year declared freedom. Both proclaimed that God owns everything—time, land, and life—and that his people live best when they trust his provision.

For Christians, these ancient rhythms still speak. We are called to rest in God's care, to forgive as we've been forgiven, and to live as a people free from fear. The God of Jubilee still invites weary souls to faith and freedom.

EXAMINATION

Rest for a restless world (25:1-2)

The laws of Leviticus 25 brought Israel's holiness to its final rhythm—the holiness of time and trust. After describing sacred days and feasts in chapter 23, and the continual light and bread in chapter 24, God now teaches his people how to live by faith across years and generations. "The Lord spoke to Moses on Mount Sinai, saying, 'Speak to the people of Israel and say to them, When you come into the land that I give you, the land shall keep a Sabbath to the Lord'" (25:1-2).

The Sabbath year and the Year of Jubilee expressed in practice what the earlier laws had symbolized: that God owns creation, sustains it, and invites his people to live in freedom and faith. The earth itself belonged to him; Israel was merely a tenant on sacred soil. These commands were not agricultural tips—they were theological declarations. The land, the people, and their labor all existed under the lordship of God.

Leviticus 25 reveals that holiness is not confined to worship or moral purity. It extends to economics, ecology, and community. Faithfulness to God includes how we rest, how we release, and how we treat those who have fallen into hardship.

The Sabbath year: Rest for the land (25:3-7)

"Six years you shall sow your field, and six years you shall prune your vineyard and gather in its fruits, but in the seventh year there shall be a Sabbath of solemn rest for the land" (25:3-4). Every seventh year, Israel was commanded to let the land rest—no plowing, sowing, or harvesting for profit. Whatever grew naturally could be eaten, but not hoarded. Even livestock and wild animals could share in the produce (25:7).

This law was radical in an agrarian economy. To rest the land meant to rest from control—to trust that God would provide enough in the sixth year to sustain them through the seventh. The Sabbath year trained Israel to remember that they were stewards, not owners. The soil, like the Sabbath day, belonged to God.

The principle reflected creation itself. Just as God rested on the seventh day, so the land rested every seventh year. Sabbath was woven into the fabric of creation, ensuring renewal for both the people and the planet.

It prevented greed, guarded against exploitation, and reminded Israel that abundance comes from grace, not endless labor.

When Israel later ignored this command, exile became the land's forced Sabbath. Second Chronicles 36:21 explains that during the Babylonian captivity, "the land enjoyed its Sabbaths." God's creation will not be exploited forever; his rhythms of rest will prevail.

For Christians, the Sabbath year calls us to ecological and spiritual stewardship. Rest is an act of faith. Whether in business, ministry, or daily life, holiness still means trusting God enough to stop and let him sustain.

The Jubilee year: Liberty and restoration (25:8–17)

If the Sabbath year was a rhythm of rest, the Jubilee was a rhythm of redemption. "You shall count seven weeks of years, seven times seven years, so that the time of the seven Sabbaths of years shall give you forty-nine years. Then you shall sound the loud trumpet on the tenth day of the seventh month. On the Day of Atonement you shall proclaim liberty throughout the land to all its inhabitants" (25:8–10).

Every fiftieth year, the trumpet signaled a nationwide reset. Debts were canceled, land returned to original families, and slaves were freed. The Hebrew word *deror* ("liberty") carries the sense of release and restoration. It was a declaration that no bondage—economic, social, or physical—was permanent among God's people.

The Jubilee taught that ultimate ownership belongs to God: "The land shall not be sold in perpetuity, for the land is mine. For you are strangers and sojourners with me" (25:23). Every sale of property was, in truth, a long-term lease until the Jubilee. This ensured that wealth could not accumulate endlessly in the hands of a few, nor could poverty trap a family forever.

The Jubilee year revealed God's compassion for the oppressed and his authority over time and possession. It was an economic manifestation of grace—a living sermon on the character of the Redeemer who liberates the captive.

Though Scripture never records Israel faithfully observing a Jubilee, the ideal remained. It became a prophetic image of the coming kingdom where God's justice and mercy would reign. Isaiah 61:1–2 proclaims that the Messiah would "proclaim liberty to the captives" and "the year of the Lord's favor." Centuries later, Jesus read that same passage in the synagogue and declared, "Today this Scripture has been fulfilled in your hearing" (Luke 4:18–21). The true Jubilee had arrived.

The theology of ownership and stewardship (25:18–24)

Both the Sabbath and Jubilee years rested on a single conviction: the land belongs to the Lord. Israel could till it, live on it, and enjoy its fruit, but never forget its owner. "The land shall not be sold in perpetuity, for the land is mine" (25:23).

This truth shaped not only economics but identity. Israel was a tenant nation, dependent on divine generosity. Holiness meant living as stewards, not sovereigns. Greed, hoarding, and exploitation violated covenant trust.

The Lord promised blessing to those who obeyed: "If you say, 'What shall we eat in the seventh year?'... I will command my blessing on you in the sixth year, so that it will produce a crop sufficient for three years" (25:20–21). God's economy was not based on anxiety but abundance. His command to rest came with the promise to provide.

This principle still governs faithful living. Everything—land, money, time, health—is on loan from God. Stewardship is not about control but gratitude. To practice holiness is to manage blessings as borrowed trust.

The call to compassion and redemption (25:25–55)

The rest of the chapter applies Sabbath and Jubilee principles to personal relationships—especially regarding debt, poverty, and servitude.

Redemption of Property and People. If an Israelite became poor and sold his land, a close relative (a *goel*, or kinsman-redeemer) could buy it back to keep it in the family (25:25). The same principle applied to people who sold themselves into servitude to survive. A redeemer could purchase their freedom, or they themselves could be released at the Jubilee (25:47–55).

The concept of redemption in Leviticus anticipates the gospel. The *goel* who restores property and freedom prefigures Christ, our Redeemer, who rescues us from bondage and restores us to our inheritance in God (Gal. 4:4–7; Eph. 1:7).

Justice for the Poor. God commanded compassion toward the poor and resident foreigners: "If your brother becomes poor and cannot maintain himself with you, you shall support him as though he were a stranger and a sojourner, and he shall live with you" (25:35). Interest could not be charged on loans to struggling Israelites (25:36–37). Holiness meant generosity without exploitation.

This law cut against every instinct of self-preservation and profit. To obey it required trust in the God who sees and rewards mercy. The Sabbath and Jubilee years thus became spiritual disciplines of compassion—a way to imitate God's gracious character.

The Value of People Over Property. Even when poverty forced someone into servitude, they were not to be treated as slaves but as hired workers and family members: "They are my servants, whom I brought out of the land of Egypt; they shall not be sold as slaves" (25:42). Ownership had limits because all people belonged to God. The memory of Egypt shaped Israel's ethics—those who had been freed must never become oppressors.

The faith that frees

The Sabbath and Jubilee laws demanded extraordinary faith. Imagine a nation resting from work every seventh year and trusting God to supply. Imagine releasing debts, freeing servants, and restoring land every fiftieth year. Obedience to such commands was an act of radical trust.

Yet God built his promises around that faith: "You shall dwell in the land securely. The land will yield its fruit, and you will eat your fill and dwell in it securely" (25:18–19). Security was not in accumulation but in obedience. Prosperity came through peace, not pressure.

This kind of faith is still countercultural. Modern life rewards hustle and hoarding, not rest and release. But the God of Leviticus still calls his people to trust his provision. Whether through Sabbath rest, financial generosity, or forgiveness, holiness begins when we stop grasping and start trusting.

Fulfillment in Christ: The true Jubilee (Luke 4:16–21)

When Jesus stood in the synagogue of Nazareth and read Isaiah 61—"He has anointed me to proclaim good news to the poor… liberty to the captives… the year of the Lord's favor"—he declared the arrival of the eternal Jubilee. In him, all the rhythms of Leviticus 25 reach their fulfillment.

- **Sabbath Rest:** Christ fulfills the rest of the land by offering rest for the soul (Matt. 11:28). In him, we cease striving and find peace.

- **Debt Forgiveness:** His blood cancels the moral debt of sin, proclaiming "It is finished."
- **Redemption:** He is the kinsman-redeemer who pays the price for our freedom and restores our inheritance.
- **Restoration:** Through the Spirit, he restores broken lives, communities, and creation itself.

In Christ, the trumpet of Jubilee still sounds. Every act of mercy, every prayer for forgiveness, and every communion meal is an echo of that liberty. The church lives as a Jubilee community, announcing that freedom has come and grace reigns.

Living the Jubilee today

The challenge for Christians is to translate the theology of Jubilee into daily practice. We do this through rhythms of rest, release, and renewal.

- **Rest:** Honor God by setting aside time to stop striving and worship. The Sabbath principle guards against idolatry of productivity.
- **Release:** Practice forgiveness, generosity, and justice. Let go of grudges and greed; release debts of the heart as God released ours.
- **Renewal:** Participate in restoring what sin has broken—relationships, families, and communities. Holiness is not retreat but renewal.

The Jubilee principle reminds the church that grace is social as well as spiritual. It renews not only souls but systems. When Christians advocate for fairness, care for creation, and lift the poor, they embody the heart of Leviticus 25—the God who loves liberty.

APPLICATION

1. Rest is an act of faith

The Sabbath year required Israel to do something extraordinary—stop working for an entire year and trust God to provide. Rest was not laziness; it was faith in action. Modern believers still need that kind of faith. We live in a world that rewards constant activity and measures worth by productivity. Yet holiness begins when we stop striving and remember that we are creatures, not creators. God calls us to rhythms of worship, stillness, and dependence. Setting aside time for rest—whether a weekly Lord's Day, a quiet morning, or a digital fast—is a declaration that he is enough. Faith rests because it trusts the Giver more than the gift. When we rest in God's provision, we rediscover the peace that no amount of effort can earn.

2. Freedom requires forgiveness

The Jubilee commanded Israel to release debts and free servants. Real freedom always involves letting go—of control, of resentment, of what others "owe" us. The same principle governs Christian life. Jesus taught his followers to forgive "as your Father forgave you." Every act of grace echoes the trumpet of Jubilee. Forgiveness doesn't erase the past, but it breaks the chain that binds us to it. When we release others from our anger, we experience our own release from bitterness. The church is meant to be a community of freedom, where mercy replaces vengeance and restoration replaces condemnation. True holiness isn't only separation from sin—it's reconciliation with others. Every time we forgive, we proclaim that grace is stronger than debt and that liberty belongs to the Lord.

3. Stewardship flows from ownership

God told Israel, "The land is mine." Everything they owned—fields, homes, harvests—was a trust, not a possession. That same truth governs Christian stewardship. We are not owners of our resources but managers of God's gifts. Whether it be money, time, or talents, everything we have belongs to him. When we live as stewards, generosity becomes natural, and greed loses its grip. The Sabbath and Jubilee laws remind us that God's kingdom values faithfulness over accumulation. Giving, serving, and sharing are not sacrifices but sacred privileges. Holiness means handling the temporary in light of the eternal. When believers treat God's blessings as tools for blessing others, they reflect the heart of the true Owner—and their lives become living testaments of gratitude.

4. Live as a Jubilee people

The trumpet of Jubilee announced liberty, restoration, and joy. In Christ, that sound still echoes through the gospel. Every believer has been released from sin's debt and invited into freedom. But the church must not only celebrate this truth—it must embody it. To live as a Jubilee people means showing the world what redeemed life looks like: generosity instead of greed, rest instead of exhaustion, forgiveness instead of revenge, and hope instead of despair. Our worship, our giving, and our compassion all proclaim that the true Year of the Lord's Favor has arrived in the person of Jesus Christ. When Christians live with open hands and joyful hearts, they become the trumpet blast of grace—a living reminder that the God of Leviticus still sets captives free.

CONCLUSION

Leviticus 25 closes Israel's holiness code with a call to trust. The Sabbath year and Jubilee year taught that God's people live by faith, not fear—by rest, not relentless striving. The land belonged to him, the people belonged to him, and their freedom came from his mercy. These laws were sermons in time, preaching that holiness means dependence and compassion.

In Christ, the true Jubilee has come. He is our rest, our redemption, and our release. The gospel trumpet still sounds, calling believers to live freely, forgive fully, and trust completely.

Next, Leviticus 26–27 will bring the book to its close, revealing the blessings of obedience, the warnings of rebellion, and the faithfulness of God's covenant love.

REFLECTION

1. What did the Sabbath year teach Israel about dependence on God's provision?
2. How did the Jubilee year reflect God's justice and compassion?
3. Why did God forbid permanent ownership of the land?
4. How did the kinsman-redeemer (*goel*) foreshadow Christ's redemptive work?
5. What connection does Leviticus 25 make between holiness and economic fairness?
6. How does Jesus fulfill the Sabbath and Jubilee in Luke 4?

DISCUSSION

1. What practices help you rest in God's provision instead of your performance?
2. How can forgiveness bring freedom to both giver and receiver?
3. In what ways can modern Christians practice Jubilee-like generosity?
4. How can we live as stewards, not owners, of God's blessings?
5. What would it look like for the church to embody Jubilee in community?
6. How does trusting God's control help you release anxiety and embrace rest?

12

BLESSING & COMMITMENT
LEVITICUS 26–27

Objective: To recognize God's covenant faithfulness and respond with obedience, repentance, and wholehearted devotion.

INTRODUCTION

In 1914, explorer Ernest Shackleton prepared for an Antarctic expedition. Before he set sail, he published a simple, striking ad: "Men wanted for hazardous journey. Low wages, bitter cold, long months of complete darkness… honor and recognition in case of success." Hundreds volunteered. They knew the risks but trusted the leader. They wanted to be part of something that mattered.

Leviticus 26–27 carries a similar call to covenant commitment. God invites his people to a life of purpose and faithfulness. The blessings and curses are not bargains but choices—will Israel walk with the God who redeemed them or turn away? Obedience would bring abundance and peace; rebellion would bring hardship and exile. Yet even in warning, God promised mercy. His covenant love would outlast their failure.

The book closes with an appeal to wholehearted devotion. True holiness is not mere rule-keeping; it is a loyal relationship. God blesses faithfulness because he delights in fellowship. He disciplines rebellion because he desires restoration. And he remembers repentance because his covenant never fails.

EXAMINATION

The covenant framework (26:1-2)

Leviticus ends not with new laws but with a covenant reminder. "You shall not make idols for yourselves or erect an image or pillar… You shall keep my Sabbaths and reverence my sanctuary: I am the Lord" (26:1-2). These opening verses summarize everything that has come before—right worship, reverence for God's holiness, and faithful obedience to his word.

Chapter 26 unfolds in the familiar covenant pattern of the ancient world: blessings for obedience, curses for disobedience, and promises of restoration. It functions as the conclusion not only to Leviticus but to the Sinai covenant itself. God's relationship with Israel was never mechanical. Obedience brought blessing not because God rewarded performance but because holiness aligned his people with his purposes. Disobedience, by contrast, fractured fellowship and unleashed the consequences of rebellion.

Chapters 26-27 thus form the book's epilogue—a call to covenant faithfulness and wholehearted devotion. They remind us that holiness is sustained not by ritual precision alone but by covenant relationship. The God who redeems expects loyalty; the people he redeems must choose whom they will serve.

Blessings of obedience (26:3-13)

"If you walk in my statutes and observe my commandments and do them…" (26:3). The blessings begin with that conditional phrase—faithful obedience. What follows is a series of cascading promises describing life under divine favor.

Fruitfulness and Peace. "I will give you rains in their season… the land shall yield its increase" (26:4). In an arid climate, rain meant life. God's blessing touched every sphere: agriculture, livestock, family, and security. "You shall eat your bread to the full and dwell in your land securely" (26:5). Obedience brought both abundance and safety.

Victory and Presence. "You shall chase your enemies, and they shall fall before you by the sword" (26:7). Israel's strength would come not from numbers but from nearness to God. "I will make my dwelling among you… and I will walk among you and will be your God, and you shall be my people" (26:11–12). That promise—echoing Eden—is the climax of blessing. The goal of obedience was always fellowship.

Freedom and Identity. "I am the Lord your God, who brought you out of the land of Egypt, that you should not be their slaves" (26:13). Obedience preserved the freedom God had already given. The liberated must remain loyal to their Liberator.

For Christians, these blessings illustrate that obedience is not transactional but transformational. The joy of faithfulness lies not in reward but in relationship. When believers walk in God's ways, they experience the peace, purpose, and fruitfulness that flow naturally from life aligned with his will.

Consequences of disobedience (26:14–39)

The second section reverses the first. Instead of fruitfulness, famine; instead of peace, panic. Yet the structure reveals a deeper truth—God's judgment is progressive and purposeful. The repeated refrain, "If you will not listen to me," marks each escalation (26:14, 18, 21, 23, 27). Discipline increases in severity not out of cruelty but in hopes of repentance.

Stage One: Fear and Frustration (26:14–17). Disobedience would bring sudden terror, disease, and defeat. "You shall sow your seed in vain, for your enemies shall eat it" (26:16). The blessings of productivity would turn into futility.

Stage Two: Drought and Hardship (26:18–20). If rebellion continued, "I will make your heavens like iron and your earth like bronze" (26:19). The imagery of hardened sky and soil depicts both divine displeasure and natural barrenness.

Stage Three: Pestilence and Plague (26:21–26). Persistent defiance would invite the full weight of covenant curse—wild beasts, sword, and famine. The phrase "I will act with hostility toward you" (26:24) expresses how rebellion transforms relationship. The God of blessing becomes the adversary of sin.

Stage Four: Devastation and Exile (26:27–39). The final escalation culminates in exile. "I myself will devastate the land... I will scatter you among the nations" (26:32–33). Israel's history confirms this outcome. When they rejected the covenant, the land enjoyed its Sabbaths while the people endured captivity (2 Chr. 36:21).

Yet even these curses reveal mercy. God's purpose was not destruction but restoration. Every judgment carried an invitation: "Then if they confess their iniquity... then I will remember my covenant" (26:40-42). Discipline in Scripture is always redemptive.

For Christians today, this passage warns that sin still carries consequences—not as divine revenge but as spiritual corrosion. God's holiness cannot coexist with rebellion. Yet even his discipline is an expression of love, calling us back to the joy of obedience.

Hope through repentance (26:40-46)

The covenant curses do not end in despair but in hope. "But if they confess their iniquity and the iniquity of their fathers... then I will remember my covenant with Jacob" (26:40-42). Restoration begins not with reform but with repentance. The Hebrew verb *zakar* ("remember") implies covenant faithfulness, not mere recollection. God does not forget his promises; he reactivates them when his people return in humility.

The key phrase appears in verse 44: "Yet for all that, when they are in the land of their enemies, I will not spurn them... for I am the Lord their God." Even in exile, grace persists. God's covenant loyalty (*hesed*) endures human unfaithfulness.

This section anticipates the message of prophets like Hosea and Jeremiah: divine discipline is never the last word. God's ultimate goal is reconciliation, not rejection.

For Christians, this passage shines with gospel light. Our hope does not rest on perfect obedience but on the faithfulness of the God who keeps covenant through Christ. The cross stands as the ultimate "I will remember." In Jesus, the curse of the covenant has been borne, and the blessings restored.

Dedication and devotion (27:1-34)

After the solemn grandeur of chapter 26, the laws about vows in chapter 27 may seem anticlimactic. But they form a fitting conclusion. Having reviewed obedience and rebellion, the book ends by reminding Israel that covenant faithfulness expresses itself through voluntary devotion.

Leviticus 27 deals with people and property dedicated to the Lord. A person might vow to give himself, a family member, or possessions in gratitude or petition. The law provided a system of valuation and redemption so that vows could be fulfilled responsibly.

The point is not accounting—it is integrity. God expected sincerity in worship. Rash vows or empty promises profaned his name as surely as idolatry did. Holiness required that what was promised be performed.

These closing laws also affirm that devotion was not limited to priests or sacrifices. Every Israelite could express consecration personally and voluntarily. The God who sanctified his people invited them to respond in love.

The chapter concludes: "These are the commandments that the Lord commanded Moses for the people of Israel on Mount Sinai" (27:34). The covenant that began with sacrifice now ends with dedication. Holiness begins with God's grace and returns to him in gratitude.

The heart of the covenant: Relationship, not rule-keeping

The twin chapters of Leviticus 26–27 distill the entire book into one message: holiness is relational. The blessings and curses are not mechanical reactions but moral realities flowing from intimacy or alienation with God. When his people walk with him, life flourishes; when they reject him, life collapses.

At its core, the covenant is a marriage of mercy and fidelity. The same God who demands loyalty also promises forgiveness. The pattern of covenant life—obedience, discipline, repentance, restoration—mirrors the rhythms of any faithful relationship. Sin strains fellowship, confession restores it, and love sustains it.

In the New Testament, this covenant is fulfilled in Christ. The blessings of Leviticus find permanence in his kingdom, and the curses find their end in his cross. The people who once trembled at Sinai now draw near to Zion, where grace and holiness meet.

Fulfillment in Christ: The faithful covenant-keeper

Every thread of Leviticus' covenant tapestry converges in Jesus.

- **Obedience and Blessing:** Christ is the only one who perfectly walked in God's statutes. Through his obedience, we receive the blessings of fellowship, peace, and fruitfulness.
- **Curse and Exile:** On the cross, he bore the covenant curses—forsakenness, suffering, and shame—so that his people might

be restored. "Christ redeemed us from the curse of the law by becoming a curse for us" (Gal. 3:13).
- **Repentance and Restoration:** His resurrection announces the renewal of the covenant, fulfilling God's promise to remember mercy.
- **Dedication and Devotion:** Christ embodies total consecration. Every vow in Leviticus 27 points to the One who gave himself completely to God's will.

Through Christ, believers become covenant partners, not covenant violators. The Spirit writes the law on our hearts, enabling joyful obedience. We no longer serve under fear of curses but in gratitude for grace.

The God of Leviticus still walks among his people—not in a tent but in the temple of the church. The covenant promise endures: "I will dwell among them and be their God, and they shall be my people."

The call to faithful commitment

Leviticus ends where holiness begins: with a choice. Will God's people walk in his ways or follow their own? The book that began with sacrifice and atonement concludes with blessing and devotion. Holiness, it turns out, is not about distance from the world but nearness to God.

The message of Leviticus 26–27 echoes through the ages: obedience brings life, rebellion brings ruin, and repentance brings restoration. The covenant remains unshakable because its foundation is the faithfulness of God.

For Christians, the call is the same—to live as covenant people in a world of broken promises. We keep the "vows" of discipleship not to earn favor but to honor the grace we've received. The covenant of Leviticus still stands fulfilled in Christ: God is faithful, his people are called to be faithful, and holiness is the harmony of both.

APPLICATION

1. Obedience flows from relationship, not obligation

The blessings of Leviticus 26 were not wages for obedience but fruits of fellowship. God promised abundance, peace, and his presence to a people who walked with him—not because they earned it, but because holiness aligns life with the Creator's design. Christians often treat obedience as duty rather than delight, but true holiness grows from gratitude, not guilt. We serve because we belong. Jesus said, "If you love me, you will keep my commandments." Love transforms rules into relationship. When we understand that obedience is how we stay close to the One who redeemed us, faithfulness becomes joy, not burden. Every act of surrender—large or small—draws us nearer to the blessing of his presence, where peace and purpose flourish together.

2. Discipline is God's mercy in disguise

The covenant warnings may sound harsh, but their purpose was restoration, not retribution. God disciplines his people because he loves them too much to let sin destroy them. The repeated refrain "If you will not listen…" reveals a patient Father calling his children home. Christians experience the same refining mercy. When our choices lead to emptiness or hardship, God's goal is not punishment but repentance. He uses pain to awaken faith, to strip away idols, and to remind us that peace cannot be found apart from him. Hebrews 12:10 says, "He disciplines us for our good, that we may share his holiness." Discipline is not rejection—it is invitation. The God who corrects also comforts, and his wounds always heal deeper than they hurt.

3. Repentance restores what rebellion ruins

When Israel confessed its sin, God promised to "remember the covenant." That word "remember" means more than recall—it means renewal. Repentance reopens the door that rebellion closed. For Christians, confession is not humiliation but liberation. It releases the soul from guilt and welcomes God's restoring grace. The same covenant faithfulness that brought Israel home from exile now brings believers back from sin's wilderness. Repentance is not a one-time event but a lifelong rhythm of return. Every honest prayer of confession becomes a new beginning. The cross guarantees that no failure is final. God's covenant mercy is stronger than our rebellion, and his grace runs deeper than our guilt. When we turn to him, the blessings once lost are not only restored—they're multiplied through Christ.

4. Devotion is the overflow of gratitude

Leviticus ends with vows and offerings—a fitting reminder that holiness concludes in devotion. After hearing of blessing and curse, Israel was invited to respond voluntarily with gifts of dedication. Gratitude always leads to generosity. For Christians, devotion means offering ourselves as "living sacrifices, holy and acceptable to God" (Rom. 12:1). Worship is not confined to a sanctuary; it's the posture of a thankful heart. We fulfill our vows to God not through ritual promises but through daily faithfulness—keeping our word, serving with humility, and giving with joy. The God who redeemed us deserves our best, not our leftovers. Holiness that begins in grace should end in gratitude. When we dedicate our time, talents, and treasure to him, we echo Israel's final act: acknowledging that everything we have belongs to the Lord.

CONCLUSION

Leviticus ends where holiness begins—with the faithfulness of God. The blessings and warnings of chapters 26–27 remind us that obedience brings life, rebellion brings loss, and repentance brings restoration. Through every stage of Israel's story, God's covenant love remained constant. He disciplines to correct, forgives to restore, and blesses to draw his people close.

For Christians, this covenant is fulfilled in Christ, the obedient Son who bore the curse so we could receive the blessing. His faithfulness becomes the foundation of ours. The call remains the same: to live as a people devoted to the God who never breaks his promises.

REFLECTION

1. What does obedience reveal about Israel's relationship with God?
2. How did God's blessings express his desire for fellowship, not reward?
3. Why were the covenant curses progressive and purposeful?
4. What role did repentance play in restoring Israel's fellowship with God?
5. How do the laws about vows reflect personal devotion and gratitude?
6. How does Christ fulfill and secure the covenant promises of Leviticus?

DISCUSSION

1. How can obedience become an expression of love rather than legalism?
2. What has God taught you through times of discipline or correction?
3. How can confession renew our relationship with God and others?
4. What practices help believers keep their hearts devoted and thankful?
5. How does the church today embody the blessings of God's covenant?
6. Which truth from Leviticus 26–27 most strengthens your trust in God's faithfulness?

www.ingramcontent.com/pod-product-compliance
Lightning Source LLC
Chambersburg PA
CBHW070151080526
44586CB00015B/1946